Love You More

Love You More

The Divine Surprise of Adopting My Daughter

Jennifer Grant

THOMAS NELSON
Since 1798

NASHVILLE   DALLAS   MEXICO CITY   RIO DE JANEIRO

Published in Nashville, Tennessee, by Thomas Nelson. Thomas Nelson is a registered trademark of Thomas Nelson, Inc.

Thomas Nelson, Inc. titles may be purchased in bulk for educational, business, fund-raising, or sales promotional use. For information, please e-mail SpecialMarkets@ThomasNelson.com.

Unless otherwise noted, Scripture quotations are taken from the New King James Version®. © 1982 by Thomas Nelson, Inc. Used by permission. All rights reserved.

Scripture quotations marked CEV are from the Contemporary English Version. © 1991 by the American Bible Society. Used by permission.

Library of Congress Cataloging-in-Publication Data

ISBN 13: 9780849946448

Printed in the United States of America

11 12 13 14 15 RRD 5 4 3 2 1

For Mia

Contents

Acknowledgments

So many people to thank before the music starts and they yank me off the stage.

First, thank you to my mom, Myrna Reid Grant, for uncountable gifts of prayer and love. Thank you to all of my Grant family—Julie and Chris Grant, Heather and Dan Hawthorne, Jillian, Meghan, and Alison Grant, and Julie and Drew Grant, Amanda and Charlie Zagnoli, Torey, Nick, and Claire Grant. When I saw the photo of all of us from Heather and Dan's wedding, I realized that God had truly made us a strong clan that will *Stand Fast*.

Thank you to Alethea and Larry Funck, generous people who don't deserve such a flat, unappealing designation as "in-laws." I'm a daughter-in-law who is fortunate to love her husband's mother and to feel unconditionally loved by her. Similarly, who knew my brother-in-law and sister-in-law would become two of my closest friends? Thank you to Brian Funck and Sara Hendren for abiding friendship—and for advice on early drafts of this book. I love you two and Graham, Winifred, and Malcolm more than I can say. Thanks to more Funcks and extended family in Pennsylvania for warmly welcoming me into the family more than two decades ago and supporting all of us during our adoption adventure—Rhoda Funck Meyer; Diane Keller, Nathan and Jenny Keller; Tom and Vivian Spahr, and Debbie and Brenda and families.

Thank you to friends who make my life so sweet. Tricia and Michael Benich—you are funny and true—and Tricia, that you told me that an early draft of this book made you laugh kept me writing on many crisis-of-confidence days. Thank you to Suzanne Ecklund for your bright spirit, dark humor, and for sermons that de-ice my heart. Thank you to Andrea Nelson LeRoy for a lifetime of friendship and for sharing Mildred—and so much more—with me. Thank you to Mark and Mary Lewis for knowing to hit the panic button when my voice gets very calm, some of the best vacations ever, and for walking along with us for so long. Olivia, Ruby, and Leah Lewis—you better know how much I love you. Thank you to Cathleen, Maury, and Vasco Possley for friendship, nicknames, and wrapping us in warmth in so many ways. Thank you to (Uncle) Jimmy Saba for being, truly, family and continuing to visit the Rumpus Suite despite the used magazines, generic bottles of water, and finding Tinker Toys in the futon. Thank you to Karen and Greg Halvorsen Schreck for your grace and support. Thank you to Magdalena and Teo Schreck for being your sweet selves. Thank you to Susan and Scott Shorney for longtime friendship—I'm grateful to be able to count Susan as a friend since "Jessie's Girl" came out. Thank you to Thaddaeus Vincent Smith for postcards, dancing bears, and the lavish way you spread jam on toast. Thank you to Kevin and Sherry Spengel for holy pastries, friendship, and welcoming so many little lives into your family, including beautiful Joe, Maria, Vinnie, and Grace. Thank you to Jon Sweeney for being my friend ever since we drove around in your dad's car listening to Lionel Richie and eating ice cream from White Hen Pantry. Thank you to Kathy and Jeremy Treat for your stunning friendship, text messages, and being excellent traveling partners. Coy and Cooper Treat and Nick and Jacob Reber—you are creative, compassionate, much-loved boys and I'm lucky to know you.

Thank you to the members of The Thread. I'm grateful to sit at this (virtual) lunch table and I love sharing the details of life every single day with you. You're the most intelligent, faithful, creative, irreverent, beautiful bunch of oddballs I've ever known.

Thank you to fellow Redbud Writers Guild members. Angie Weszely, Anita Lustrea, Arloa Sutter, Caryn Dahlstrand Rivadeneira, Helen Lee, Karen Halvorsen Schreck, Keri Wyatt Kent, Melinda Schmidt, Princess Zulu, Shayne Moore, Suanne Camfield, and Tracey Biachi—it's not possible to measure the influence you've had on my work. I am proud to be counted among you. (And I'm just plain fond of you.)

Thank you to the people who have been Mia's cherished teachers, caregivers, and supporters, including Norma Cid, Wilma Linde, Linda Chase, Heather Kotula, Ariel Woodiwiss, Paul McKinney, Katie Ekstrand, Kim Swanson, Dianne Thornburg, Esther Harris, Barbara Anderson, Kylie Strating, Michele Gorman, Kathleen Leid, and Claire Siemer.

Thank you to my church family at St. Mark's Episcopal Church in Glen Ellyn, especially Laurie Vanderlei for encouragement, love, and making it possible for us to meet Mia when she was still a baby, and to Catharine Phillips for prayers, poems, and friendship. Thank you to Adrian and Trey Buchanan, Joyce and David Fletcher, Elizabeth and Leo Lanzillo, and Cecilia and George Smith for journeying through happy—and very hard—times with us so faithfully.

Thank you to Susie Lane for the gift of letting me experience Vermont in October and, thereby, helping me to finish this book.

Thank you to my brother and agent Chris Grant for being

extremely gifted at both. Thank you to Julie Busteed for tenaciously circulating the proposal that would grow into this book.

Thank you to Matt Baugher and Debbie Wickwire, who warmly welcomed me to Thomas Nelson. Thank you to Jennifer Stair for your precision and all you did to help me tell this story more clearly.

Finally, thank you to my dearest ones. Thank you, David, for taking me to the Wheaton Grand when I was twenty and telling me you wanted to marry me three weeks later. I love sharing this life with you—what a story it continues to make. Theo, Ian, Isabel, and Mia—you are my treasures.

I love you (more).

A Conspicuous Family

I t's just life. One moment I'm standing in the frozen foods aisle, looking for puff pastry sheets or a bag of chopped spinach and the next I'm fielding a delicate question from a stranger about my family or my reproductive health. "When you become the parents of a child of another race, you become a conspicuous family," the social worker had said when my husband and I began the adoption process. "Are you ready for that?" I said I was, but it still throws me that seeing my family can have the effect of causing perfectly well-mannered people to turn off their filters and use their "outside voices" to express whatever thoughts pop into their heads.

"Couldn't you have another one of your own?"

"Where did you get her?"

"How much was she?"

"Have you ever met her real mother?"

"Does she speak English?"

Without exception, the curious, frozen-lima-bean-buying stranger's tone quickly changes from alarmed to friendly when I answer her question. I adopted Mia when she was a toddler, I explain. She was born in Guatemala. She belongs to me as much as my three older children, to whom I gave birth, do. Often the person who blurted out her question reveals that she has a sister, a neighbor, or a friend who is considering adoption. We chat a bit, she smiles at Mia and says how beautiful she is, and we go our separate ways. I then try to remember what I was looking for in the first place. Frozen blueberries? Pizza? Edamame?

I only felt bruised by a stranger's comments once. It wasn't so much what he said, but his icy tone that bothered me. He stood in line ahead of me at the post office, turned and regarded my four children, and said, "One of them doesn't match." Fortunately, my kids were too young or too distracted by the display of commemorative Elvis stamps to have heard him. The man continued to stare at us until a clerk called out the number printed on the tag in his hand. At first, his comment and his disapproving glare felt like a kick in the stomach, but by the time he was walking out of the post office, I was smiling to myself. I have a secret that protects my heart from people like him: even if the members of my family don't "match," we are perfectly coordinated, chosen to be together. I have no doubt about it.

Anna Karenina is my favorite novel, bar none, but it begins with a lousy first sentence. With easy authority, Tolstoy writes, "Happy families are all alike; every unhappy family is unhappy in its own way." Every time my eyes pass over those first fourteen words, a buzzer goes off in my head. Actually, it is less a buzzer and more like someone has struck Chuck Barris's big brass gong. (Remember *The Gong Show?* "Gene, Gene the Dancing Machine?") My point is that when I read "happy families are all alike," I know it is just not true.

That statement sounds so permanent, so definitive, so set. Life's not like that. Families are ever in process, ducking and taking cover during times of grief and hardship and casually strolling through easier times, forgetting to notice how fortunate they are. Things change, flip horizontally, upend themselves.

On ordinary days, as well as on life-changing ones, just when we think we know what our lives are like, things change. And our pliable, stretchy hearts strain to take it all in. We scramble to figure out what will be the new normal from then on.

Take caring for a baby, for example. From five to seven every evening for what feels like a year, your baby wails. It's a swirling cycle of fury and woe that you're nearly certain has cost you your eardrums. Every night you and your spouse take turns eating whatever meal one of you has managed to prepare. Dinner at your place, pre-baby, was gourmet. Now you are living on the kinds of meals most often found on a kids menu. At a pancake house. Then one day, you open the doorway jumper that the neighbor gave you as a shower gift. You hang it up and test it several thousand times with phone books and stuffed animals. After it has met your safety inspection, you lower the screaming baby into it. The baby looks shocked and you fear he will only cry harder. You give it a hesitant bounce and then the unthinkable happens: he stops crying.

You and your husband look at each other. You scrape the untouched applesauce and macaroni and cheese off your plates and take some real food out of the refrigerator. Arugula. Goat cheese. Balsamic vinegar. For the next two hours, you and your husband linger over dinner, talk about topics unrelated to colic, and can barely believe your luck.

Ah, you think. *The hard bit is over.*

You have it all figured out.

But things change, don't they? After three glorious weeks, you glance over at the baby during dinner and see that he is climbing out of the jumper. He has one leg completely freed and is careening quickly toward the ground. You drop your fork, catch him just before his head makes contact with the floor, and spend the next half hour reconsidering your position on playpens . . . and on parenthood in general.

Why did we do this thing again?

Life never stops changing. It's a challenge even when everything goes reasonably well and tragedy hasn't struck your family, violently tearing it apart the way lightning can split trees in a storm.

So, Mr. Tolstoy, as much as I adore Anna's story and marvel at the depth of the characters who surround her, I wonder how you could make such a statement about families, happy or otherwise. It's a statement that suggests that families can be categorized simply, evaluated from outside. But you cannot know what is going on inside of someone's home unless you are deep on the inside and unless it is your own.

Maybe a family is conspicuous and maybe it doesn't seem to "match." Indeed, increasingly, families come in all shapes, shades, and sizes. But for better and worse, each family is certainly happy—and unhappy—in its own way. What's more, I don't think families ever fit so tidily into either a "happy" or "unhappy" column. Happiness is a fluid thing, isn't it? Doesn't it go in cycles? It certainly has in my experience.

Expanding my family by adoption pushed me into uncomfortable places, challenged my notions about what family means, and brought abiding happiness. Like all true ones, my story is comprised of joyful moments and times of deep longing and pain. Adoption was new to me. As an optimist who was confident in her parenting skills, I only half-listened to warnings from professionals about everything from the unpredictability of the adoption process to the grief my new baby might experience after being separated from her foster family. (*Sure, sure. Maybe she will miss them a bit at first, but they were never her real family. For them, it was just a job.*) I nodded solemnly at all the cautionary tales, but I entered into the process expecting that our case would go quickly, she would attach quickly, and all would be well. Quickly.

After all, the decision to adopt was not my idea, really. I was merely responding to a tap on the shoulder from God. I was sure of it. Wouldn't God, then, expedite the whole thing? I knew God could. But Mia's adoption ran into snags. Documents had to be checked, again and again. Holidays closed down courts and businesses for days and sometimes weeks. These delays were not even comparable to what parents who adopt from China or Nepal have experienced over the past few years. There was no intergovernmental red tape or uncertainty going on in our adoption, just lawyers and judges doing their jobs. (Anyway, wasn't it me who researched ethical violations in Guatemalan adoptions and wanted to be as certain as I could that ours was legitimate? Shouldn't I have been *grateful* that everyone was being so attentive to detail?) Somewhere along the line, however, it was no longer about obedience to God or respecting a careful process. I had fallen in love with the daughter I hadn't even met.

And I had to wait. But wasn't God aware that waiting wasn't my specialty? Didn't God recall that I was the one who always cut the classes I found dull? That I was a champion skimmer of textbooks and instruction booklets? That I grew restless in boring meetings? I liked doing things my way. Thinking fast. Making things happen. Skipping to the good parts.

When something was too tedious, no matter what its ultimate benefits would be, I quickly pulled the plug on it. Like when

I was in high school and, summer after summer, I would commit to myself that this year I'd get a killer tan. Some of my friends had great success "laying out." (That's what we called it in Chicagoland in the early 1980s.) Sure, I knew that it would require that I lie motionless, slathered in baby oil on an uncomfortable lawn chair in the backyard for hours, turning every so often so that the backs of my arms and legs would be equally browned.

I knew I'd be hot, and I don't like being hot. I knew I'd be working against nature—my Scottish ancestry hasn't provided me with skin that responds well to sun. I knew that the glaring sun and potential for damaging a beloved book would keep me from my favorite pastime. Nevertheless, I figured I could do it this time. Become Coppertone Jen.

The first time out, I lay there, skin greasy and gleaming, for what seemed like hours. Decades. Epochs. I listened to faraway sounds such as the buzz of lawnmowers or the warble of the ice cream truck, playing "The Entertainer" over and over as it wound through town. I tried to persuade myself that this was pleasant, frittering away the hours like this. Then, pleased with my tenacity and certain that I was halfway to Bo Derek brown, I roused myself from the lawn chair. I figured that the sun might be setting soon. It was probably even time for dinner. I went inside the house to check the time, shaking the sweat from my hair. As my eyes adjusted to light inside the house, I looked at the clock and was astonished. At most, four or five minutes had elapsed since I had first dragged the lawn chair into the sun. The experience was so mind-numbingly dull that I wouldn't try again until the following summer. Year after year, I did no better in my quest to be sun-kissed. Finally, I gave up and accepted my chicken-breast-under-cellophane-in-the-refrigerated-section-of-the-grocery-store pallor. If

I could not stand a few hours of lying on a folding lawn chair in the sun in hopes of a tan, imagine my impatience waiting for the child I loved. (If you are an adoptive parent, whether you waited weeks or years to bring your child home, you understand.)

By the time she finally arrived home, Mia was no longer a baby but a toddler who suddenly found herself in a house full of people who did not speak her language. We looked different from anyone she had ever known. She now had siblings who were young, loud, and possessive of their mother. And the food? It wasn't until a week or two after her homecoming that my husband brought home black bean burritos for dinner. I was still setting out the plates when I noticed Mia. She was sitting up straight in her high chair eating the beans I had spooned onto her tray as though they were a delicacy. She looked relieved, as if finally someone had served her some *real* food. That night I saw her eat like I had never seen her eat before.

"You can keep your quiches, your pasta, and that tofu stir fry," she seemed to say. "*This* is what I'm talking about!"

People ask me how well she adjusted after she came home. "She did fine," I say with a sigh. "I was the one who had trouble." When I explain that, regardless of whether I'd adopted Mia or she had come into the family the traditional way, I was destined to rise to the level of my incompetence with my fourth child, I am only half-joking. The truth is, Mia did a much better job of adjusting to her new family, home, and culture than I did adjusting to having four children and becoming a mother by adoption. I second-guessed myself. I had unrealistic expectations of myself and of her. I kept most of my fears secret. I half-believed the irrational ideas that had crept into my consciousness during the months of waiting. One was that, despite her age and the culture shock,

Mia would realize, almost immediately, that we were people to be trusted, that she had arrived home, and that God had this arrangement in mind from the dawn of time. I think I almost expected that she would understand what I had been through, waiting for her. You would think I would have known better, right? I was a parenting columnist for a newspaper, immersed in research about everything from creating age-appropriate birthday parties to disciplining children effectively. I was the mother of three young children and well versed in child development. I had read all of the adoption books I could find. On bad days, however, I somehow expected Mia to be some kind of toddler psychic.

"You have just been through something rather traumatic," the ideal Mia-toddler would say, after taking a long sip of apple juice from her juice box. "It must have been awful for you, waiting for me like that. You're not much good at long-suffering, are you? Or so I hear. Let me just say that I'm glad to finally be home. All the expense and emotional strain has been worth it. It'll all be smooth sailing from here on out, okay?"

People ask me if I loved Mia right away and whether I love her as much as the children to whom I gave birth. Yes, on both counts. I've experienced that rush of love in different ways with each of my four, and yes, I loved her right away. Because that was my experience with Mia, however, does not mean it is how all parents feel. Many people I know who have more than one child admit to relating more deeply with one or more of their children from the start. They confess that it takes more time or more of an effort to connect with others. Regardless of whether a child was born to them or came to them by adoption, not all parents feel an immediate bond with their children. Some women who have just given birth take a long look at the little stranger who has been placed into their arms and think, *Really? This is what all the trouble was for?* (I know they do; they have told me.)

It is often our expectations that make us stumble. Sometimes a woman imagines that just after birth, maybe right after the umbilical cord is cut, her newborn will be Gerber-baby cute and might even giggle at a game of peekaboo. Such parents have seen the chubby babies in movies or on television, the ones who lie in acrylic bassinets in the newborn nursery. Those babies are nearly ready, developmentally, to sit up, lower themselves down to the floor, and crawl somewhere to find a sippy cup. (Between takes, you can almost hear the baby actors shouting, "Hey! Somebody call craft services. I told my agent I only drink artesian well water. What is this swill?") The point is, some new moms look at their extremely small and wrinkly newborns and feel . . . disappointed. Give it a few months. When a baby starts to sleep through the night or when his face lights up when he sees you standing over his crib, it is next to impossible not to fall madly in love with him.

Similarly, some parents who have adopted their children dare not confess that it took time to feel the kind of genuine love they now have for them. Such parents have scoured their homes and lives in preparation for the home study. They have sufficiently proved what loving and capable parents they will be. No spanking. Consistently enforced time-outs. Limited television. Lots of reading together. Daily outdoor play. Mozart on the radio. Organic strawberries. Nontoxic, eco-friendly cleaning supplies. Hm . . . what else? The wipes will always be gently warmed, the bottles never heated in the microwave, and only a few grains of refined sugar will pass over their children's lips every year. (Phew—did we get all the answers right?) Their friends and clergy have written long letters extolling their virtues. They have opened their medical files and financial statements to the world, and everyone from the local police to the FBI has verified that they are not criminals. (They do not even have unpaid parking tickets and they never, ever jaywalked.) They have weathered the disapproval of unsupportive family or friends and the ambivalence of wary employers. They have shrugged off the barrage of inappropriate questions and remarks.

Many have also gone through the physical and emotional pain of infertility.

By the way, if your friend or coworker (or anyone) tells you that she is adopting a child, never respond by saying that if she will merely do a headstand after having intercourse, she will get pregnant. (Do not ask her if she has tried that yet. Really.) Likewise, do not say that the minute she starts filling out the forms to adopt, she will find out she is pregnant. You may mean well by saying these things, but I have it on very good information that these comments are not useful. Just give her a hug and say, "Congratulations."

So do you think, after enduring all of the above, a person who has just adopted a child is going to say, "You know, I'm not sure I like this kid" or "I'm questioning whether I really want to be a parent after all"?

You tell me.

Sadly, adoptive parents sometimes think that if they do not feel an immediate bond with the child who is now legally theirs, it has something to do with the way their child came into the family. It is not. I once wrote a newspaper column about attachment in parenting and interviewed about a dozen mothers. Some had adopted their kids; some had given birth to them. Their comments confirmed that it is normal to feel an immediate bond with your child and it is just as normal *not* to experience it for a while. It did not matter whether the mom had gone through labor and given birth to the baby or had welcomed her child by adoption. It was evenly split among the "it took time" and the "when I laid eyes on her, I was in love" groups of mothers.

Perhaps because she was my fourth child and I was already very entrenched as a mother, I quickly felt attached to Mia after her adoption was finalized. I was aware that, in this great big world, she had no one but my husband and me to protect her, to nurture her, and to be her family. Not only did she have no one, but she had almost nothing when her foster mother placed her in our arms. She only owned the clothes on her body and the blanket I begged her foster mother to give to us. "Please explain," I said to the translator. "This blanket will be the baby's only familiar thing. Please ask if we can take it with us. It will comfort her." I had seen Mia with the pink blanket over the months in the pictures our agency sent to us. I saw the way she held a corner of it, and I knew it was her "lovey."

I knew a thing or two about loveys after all three of my older ones bonded with theirs. My oldest had a quilt made by a friend, my younger son a stuffed horse, and my daughter a soft blanket and pink rag doll. I had learned that you could no more choose what lovey your child would glom on to than choose the color of his eyes.

When my oldest rejected the quilt I had sewn in a rare fit of domesticity during my pregnancy, I shrugged. I would simply give it to my next child. Next time, I would plan ahead. I would get my quilt in the baby's crib early, stroke the baby's face with it, and hand it to him or her during thunderstorms or just before we went to the pediatrician for shots. ("Here—take this quilt. It will help.") My second child, however, also had no interest in said quilt. The same was true with my third. I knew from experience, then, that I could buy Mia many things, but I could not replace her lovey. Happily, her foster mother let me take it.

But other than the clothes on her back and that blanket, she had nothing. None of the toys, photo albums, or clothes we had sent to her over the past several months came home with us. Mia's foster mother knew that more babies would come into her home and that she would need those things. She knew we could easily replace them in the United States, so she sent Mia back with us to our hotel in old, ill-fitting clothes and shoes that were three sizes too small. Once we were in our room, however, I decked her out in a beautiful new outfit I had bought for her. It delighted me to dress her in beautiful clothes, give her new toys, and cover her with kisses. I wanted to make up for lost time after having missed the first sixteen months of her life.

Adopting Mia opened up the world to me in new ways. I look at my little girl, with her sophisticated (and sometimes extremely silly) sense of humor, her love of the natural world, and her talent for making beautiful pastel drawings. I see her sweetness and the light she brings to those around her. She began as a "waiting child" in Guatemala, but if she is of such infinite value, what about other children born to other very poor mothers around the world? Half of the world's children are born into poverty. There are an estimated 150 to 170 million orphans globally who live without parental care, are warehoused in orphanages, or live on the streets or in child-headed households.[1] Their potential is unseen, like a paper sack of daffodil bulbs hidden behind a watering can in the garage, shriveling in the dark.

These children starve to death. They die of preventable diseases. They are abused and exploited in unimaginable ways. There is a global orphan crisis; it is a pandemic.

Do I have any responsibility to these children, even though (as was the case with my Mia) I did not bring them into the world? Are they, in some mystical way, my family too? After adopting my daughter, I have come to think they are. Actually, as a mother, a person of faith, and someone who has had the privilege—and, concurrently, has been given the burden—of visiting some of the world's poorest places, I am sure of it.

Since my daughter's homecoming seven years ago, I have begun to wonder whether God has an additional purpose in bringing families together by adoption. Whether parents welcome a child who was born twenty miles from their home or was born half a world away, adoption changes the way adoptive parents perceive people with whom they may feel they have little in common. Some of us no longer view drug-addicted women who, after giving birth, leave their newborn babies at Safe Haven facilities such as hospitals and police stations as second-class citizens or pariahs. How can we not cherish them? They are our children's birthmothers. For the first time, now that we are family, we might feel a desire to explore ways to bring healing, education, and dignity to these women. Indigenous women weaving colorful fabrics in Latin America and living in poverty are no longer curiosities pictured in *National Geographic* but our children's first mothers. How can we, who now know their strength and stories, fail to help them rise out of the poverty that forces them into a desperate place, a place where they must relinquish their babies?

Is adoption—whether domestic or international—a means

by which God opens our eyes to the needs of the world and calls us to love others more?

This book, *Love You More*, is the story of how God brings families together and makes broken things whole. It is also about broadening the image of what family looks like. No, we may not all "match" as families did in 1950s advertisements for laundry powder and chewing gum. We might have very different backgrounds. We might be a conspicuous family that draws the gaze of strangers. Whatever we look like from the outside, it is a beautiful mystery that a jumbled little gathering of individuals— whether or not they are related by blood—become, truly, family.

The phrase "Love you more" is often said in my home. It is a response to "I love you," a nod to the abundance of feeling we have for one another and an affectionate game. After I switch off the light in my son's bedroom and pull the door closed, I hear a muffled "more." I open the door a crack and whisper the word back to him, then shut the door quickly and hurry down the hall. A moment later, I hear his door open. "More!" he calls. Later, I slide a note under his door. He will notice it in the morning. "*Love you more,*" it reads.

I hope that my story will encourage adoptive families, educate others about the adoption process, spark conversation about how adoption can be a first step toward investing in the communities where our children were born, and finally, serve as a happy reminder to children who were adopted, including my own, that they are loved more than they can imagine.

Part One
Starting the Journey

1

Mowing the Lawn
in the Dark

My husband and I were in the weeds.

With three children born within three and a half years, we were in constant motion, changing diapers, filling sippy cups, and snapping and unsnapping the shallow little snaps on baby clothes. There was Play-Doh in the cracks between the floorboards, and the sand from the turtle sandbox out back was slowly finding its way into the house, sockful by tiny sockful. We could not remember what it felt like to sleep late or to spend a whole Saturday morning drinking coffee and reading the paper.

Our transition from young marrieds living in New York City to new parents living in a ranch house in the suburbs of Chicago had been abrupt. After graduate school, we had moved to New York so that my husband could pursue a career as a stage actor. His master's degree, from a highly respected program, was in acting performance. In New York, he did occasional voiceovers and performed in plays, staged readings, and backers' auditions.

When David wasn't acting, he worked part-time as a tutor, taking the subway to places as far-flung as Coney Island and the Bronx. His preferred place to meet with students was at the World Trade Center's Winter Garden. A few years later, he could barely make himself look at images of the garden, buried in debris. It had been his escape in a difficult time of life, a period in which he disappointed and second-guessed himself. When he wasn't working, he was sitting on the end of our bed, staring at the wall, waiting for his agent to call. For the first time in his life, he knew what it meant to be depressed.

Meanwhile, I had a job I loved in New York. I worked for a nonprofit organization in Manhattan dedicated to improving the health of people in the world's poorest places. My job provided me with a regular paycheck, an education about global issues, and an opportunity to meet like-minded friends. It also required me to travel. Travel is my secret passion, the only luxury I long for, an itch in my soul that begs to be scratched.

David and I lived on Sterling Place in Prospect Heights, Brooklyn. "Off Flatbush, between Vanderbilt and Underhill." I gave those shorthand directions countless times to cab drivers and friends. "Prospect Heights." Even typing the name of the neighborhood makes me smile. As young, married twenty-somethings, fresh out of graduate school and renting an apartment in a grand old brownstone, my husband and I were ready to lay hold of bright futures. There we were in the aptly named neighborhood.

Were we indeed at the height of our prospects?

At the time, I did not attach any special meaning to the name. I only knew that in Brooklyn, Park Slope next door was the trendy neighborhood *du jour* with its historic homes, natural foods stores, top-rated restaurants, and of course, massive Prospect

Park. The park was created by Frederick Law Olmsted and Calvert Vaux, the men who designed Central Park in Manhattan.

I preferred the less flashy Prospect Heights to Park Slope. I liked that many of the families who lived on our block were rooted; they were there to stay. The neighborhood was diverse, middle class, and real. I felt more at home in New York than anywhere I have lived, before or since. Down the street, a few blocks east of where we lived, is Tom's Restaurant. The first time we were invited to breakfast there with friends, I realized I was about to visit an institution, a real Brooklyn gem. "They give you coffee and cookies and oranges when you're waiting in line," our friend said. "Gus, the owner, he's a *mensch*."

Tom's opened in 1936, and its décor goes back decades. There are bouquets of plastic flowers in cheap vases and kitschy paintings and strands of white lights on the wall. Signs drawn on neon poster board cutouts advertise specialties like the Cherry-Lime Ricky, egg creams, and pancake specials. "Breakfast Served All Day," they promise. There are framed family photos at the register. The waitstaff is actually friendly. Walking down the street and eating at Tom's gave me a satisfying peek into what living in the 1950s might have been like, at breakfast anyway. Tom's stirred up a longing in me for a simpler time, much the way watching an old musical does. I realize that if you were, say, the Rosenbergs, Arthur Miller, or Rosa Parks you probably would not wax eloquent about what a lovely and simple time it was in America in the 1950s. But Tom's made me feel nostalgic for artifacts of that time. Lime Rickys. A soda fountain. Courteous waiters politely chatting with you.

After a breakfast of scrambled eggs, pancakes, grits, and too much coffee, my husband and I would walk over to the farmers' market at nearby Grand Army Plaza. We lingered over fiddlehead ferns, local honey, and Ginger Gold apples. I bought milk in thick, glass bottles and returned home feeling very pleased with life's simple pleasures. A brown paper sack of mushrooms. A loaf of fresh bread. A bunch of muddy beets.

I remember one day after breakfast at Tom's, my husband and I sat out in the garden behind our apartment on a quilt, reading the newspaper. Our dog sniffed around the edges of the yard. The sky was a clear blue and I watched butterflies landing on the deep green leaves of the wisteria that braided itself through the old wooden fence. Then, in a sudden, unexpected moment, a thought knocked into me like a blow to the chest.

"I miss our children," I said aloud. "I'm homesick for them. I wish they were here with us, out here today."

I don't remember David's response, but he probably laughed and made a crotchety comment about how having a dog was hassle enough. He wanted children someday, but not yet. He certainly did not miss them in advance of their arrival. I'd ache for my—yet unknown—children again and again over the next few years, the feeling coming over me as unexpectedly and violently as it did the first time.

When I thought about being a mother, I wondered whether we would be able to conceive. Getting pregnant was no longer a given for many couples; infertility seemed to be on the rise. If we did have children, how many would we have? What would they be like? Look like? I looked at my husband's fair hair, his blue eyes and strong features, and wondered if our children would be blond. Or would they have hair as dark and unruly as my own? That day in our backyard, I pictured two small children quietly lying between us on the quilt. Maybe one would be gazing up at the sky while the other raked little fingers through the grass.

Whenever the thought of their absence hit me, I felt a gnawing pain in my chest.

I was not, however, eager to leave our life in New York, despite these occasional maternal attacks and my husband's growing dissatisfaction with the city. My life felt like an adventure. I began working on a project in Southeast Asia and flew from New York to Bangkok to work in my organization's Thailand office.

I made trips to Vietnam, first to Hanoi and then to project sites around the country. On one trip, I arrived in the city of Huế (pronounced something like "h'way"), in central Vietnam, without a driver or translator. The challenge of finding transport into the city from the airport thrilled me. I opted for a ride from two young men who, grinning, pointed at their ancient black Soviet Lada and opened the back door for me. The floor of the car had rusted through, so I sat cross-legged on the seat, clutching my briefcase in my lap, and let the lush scenery sweep by on the short ride: The beauty of the rice paddies, dotted with women bent over the fields wearing their conical hats. The water buffalo, somber-faced and massive, standing as though they were waiting to be told what to do next. People, laden with overflowing baskets of rice and sweet potatoes, walking along the side of the road toward the market.

I fell in love with Huế. Wandering around the Forbidden City was like waking up in the film *The Last Emperor*. It was magical to be in a place where cultures and histories overlapped. Some of the huge urns and statues of dragons had been marred with bullet holes, wounds sustained during the Tet Offensive when Vietnam and the United States were at war. I also couldn't spend enough time at the royal tombs Huế, their courtyards populated by neat rows of stone elephants, horses, and warriors. My favorite was the tomb of Tự Đức and the stunning gardens that surround it. In some of the bookstalls and souvenir shops, cassette tapes of traditional Vietnamese music played. Buddhist monks, dressed in saffron-colored robes, chanted. Everything was strange and captivating to me, and I had the electrifying insight that I was, truly, on the other side of the world.

I also loved Hanoi. Its energy, the narrow, winding side streets, and the vendors on the sidewalks crouching beside huge stacks of plastic chairs or pyramids constructed of fresh oranges. The streets were jammed with scooters, bikes, and cyclos. On one trip to Vietnam, I wondered whether there was a spiritual reason for these journeys. I felt a connection to the place. Why did it feel so deep? Was I meant to live here someday? Might we adopt a child from Vietnam in the future? I witnessed the poverty, I heard stories about crowded orphanages, and I had grown to love the good humor and gracious spirit of the people.

● ● ●

Back in New York, there was an on-site day care down the hall from my cubicle. I watched parents stop in multiple times a day to visit their kids. Mothers nursed their infants. Fathers slipped in to hug their children on their way to the conference room. Although I had always imagined I would be an at-home mother, I realized there were more good ways than one to raise kids. I could keep my job and be close to my baby all day when the time came.

Then, as will happen in life, everything changed.

David no longer wanted to wait out the slow momentum his career was gathering. He tired of doing what he darkly called "friends' theater," or collaborating with friends on everything from writing a script to constructing the set to printing the programs and then performing the show for an audience comprised of . . . friends. Although not many of his jobs fell into the category of "friends' theater," he had tired of living as an actor in New York. Work was coming too slowly and in fragments. David wanted what he called "a real job." He had become uncomfortably aware that he was almost thirty and that he not only wanted to have kids, but he wanted to be able to provide a comfortable, stable home for them. He started to have panic attacks.

"It's a man thing," I said, when friends expressed bewilderment about his sudden career change.

In a moment of decisiveness, we decided to return to Illinois, several years after leaving it. We moved back to the town where we both had grown up, close to where much of our family lives. David got a job in software. We bought a house and outfitted the garage with snow shovels, a lawnmower, and two cars. Within weeks, I learned that I was pregnant. Suddenly, my husband was the one with the full-time job. I spent my days padding around the house in my socks, doing laundry, paging through cookbooks, and reading volume after volume of pregnancy and parenting books. As our baby grew inside me, I pined for New York. I missed my friends. I missed my job. I missed real bagels, restaurants that stayed open past nine, and the noise and color of neighborhood festivals and street fairs. I missed walking to church on Sunday mornings over uneven slate sidewalks and missed our old parish's West Indian congregation. I missed taking a taxi to the airport and making the long journey to the other side of the world to stop in on Emperor Tự Đức or eat soft-shelled crabs in a shack on the South China Sea.

I even missed the car alarms that woke me many times on Sterling Place. Sometimes I would walk around my quiet house, singing out the long symphony of buzzers and tones that used to irritate me.

At night in the new house, listening out my open window, all I could hear were crickets.

The conversations my husband and I had begun to engage in had plummeted from heady discussions about *Waiting for Godot* ("Why do you think only Vladimir remembers things from one day to the next?") to the banal ("Should we go with the PPO, EPO, or HMO this year?"). I'd gone from a life where I might find myself drinking a bowl of chocolate and nonchalantly glancing at Uma Thurman sitting a few tables over in a Greenwich Village coffee shop to standing in a long line to apply for membership at Costco. As tender as were my feelings toward my babies, I started to feel that I was changing into a lackluster suburban mom with a long to-do list and dark circles under her eyes.

It wasn't that I didn't connect with motherhood. I had always wanted to be a mother. I remembered the yearning I'd had, back in Brooklyn, for those children who were to come. I loved so much about the first years of my children's lives. Reading books. Letting them make detours on our walks so that they could break off a flower from a lilac bush or stop and watch a train go by. "You've got to be a parent someday. If for no other reason, it's worth it for the bugs," I said to a young friend recently. Crouching on the sidewalk with your toddler to watch regiments of ants marching single file, transporting their obscenely outsized cargo. Learning about praying mantises, marveling at the aquarium of walking sticks at a nature center, counting the legs of a spider. I drank it all in.

But I wondered whether I would like the person I was turning out to be. What was happening to my brain?

After watching the movie for about the tenth time with my son, I found myself obsessing over *Chitty Chitty Bang Bang* (or "Chee Chee Bon Bon," as he called it). *What could it mean?* I'd wonder, as he danced around the room singing about Truly Scrumptious. *Truly Scrumptious?* Who has a name like that? What would my critical theory professor from graduate school make of it? I mused over the sexual politics of the song "You're My Little Chu-chi Face." I sardonically wondered whether Truly indeed was just a doll on a music box. Why wasn't anyone writing academic papers about this film? I would do it myself, I thought, if I weren't so busy winding up the baby swing and raking through the LEGO bin trying to find Darth Vader's light saber or that red headlight my son was missing.

Who was I becoming? My friend Caryn Rivadeneira has written about the complicated feelings women have about motherhood. Like me, she is in love with her children and is truly grateful to be a mother. Rivadeneira admits, however, to experiencing some quite tangled feelings about the child-rearing years.

"When being a mom looms so large that it obscures everything else God has made me to be, I sort of hate it," she has written. "Other people are not seeing the real me. Instead they see 'career mom' or 'preschool mom' or 'smiling-and-waiting-for-the-bus mom.'"[1]

I felt a growing distance from the "real" me. Now it was the "at-home-mom" me—not my husband—sitting at the end of the bed sometimes, wondering who I was, fearing that all of the layers, all of the complexity, all of the amazing life experiences I'd had in the past decade were being efficiently wiped up and folded into a paper towel, like somebody's spilled milk. Would I find myself, a few years down the line, chattering incessantly about my new granite countertops or griping about the lawn service? Would I be a woman who spends her days fretting over whether her son is popular or her daughter is the captain of the dance team? Was it inevitable?

Bruce Cockburn's song from the early 1980s, "The Trouble with Normal," played in my mind when I found myself regarding the suburban landscape and noticing things such as my neighbor's improved driveway and suddenly wondering whether we should get ours repaved too. What about those sprawling yew bushes out in front of our house? Everyone seemed to be ripping them out and putting in tidy boxwoods. Should we do that too? And was I handicapping my three-year-old son by not finding him a private batting coach or enrolling him in French lessons?

The trouble with normal—or keeping up with the Joneses—is it always gets worse.

Moreover, all David and I seemed to be doing were chores. Mopping the floor. Raking leaves. Sweeping out the garage. Washing and folding laundry. Filling a crack in the wall. Loading and unloading the dishwasher. One night a friend whom we'd known in New York, who had left the city about the same time as we did to raise his kids in the suburbs, called my husband. I answered the phone.

"Can he call you back, Paul? He's outside, mowing the lawn," I said.

"But it's almost ten," he said, and then we both dissolved into laughter at the familiar predicament of having young children and too many things to do in a day.

"Mowing the lawn in the dark" became a catchphrase for us, aptly describing our lives.

2

The Best Laid Plans

David and I had talked about adopting a child for much of our married life. Our tentative plan was to have a baby or two the traditional way. If, after that, we decided we wanted more children, we would adopt. I read that the most successful families space their children three years apart. If this would curb sibling rivalry, reduce our stress as parents, and was the best practice, I was glad to comply. (*If this was the recipe for happy and well-adjusted children, why didn't everyone space their children this way? Come on people, pay attention!*)

About nine months after we left New York, I gave birth to our first child. After our son was born, I suffered—if you can call it suffering—what my husband termed "postpartum elation." I had done it. I had brought a beautiful new human being into the world. We named him Theodore, meaning "gift of God." I was deeply grateful to have received this gift and to be a mother.

I remember looking out the window on the ride home from the hospital. Why was everyone going about their lives as though nothing had happened? The world had changed; a new little person had arrived and transformed the planet forever. Scrunched in that car seat was a tiny baby boy who might grow up to find a cure for cancer, might inspire generations by his vision and leadership, or might create magnificent works of art. There he was, tightly swaddled and strapped into the rear-facing car seat in the back of our car, bursting with promise. I thought the streets should have been lined with people, not only to mark his homecoming but to celebrate every new life who exited that hospital driveway. The hope, potential, and love that could grow from this tiny person felt almost overwhelming to me.

(Yes, I was a first-time mother.)

When Theo was several months old, our health insurance plan changed, necessitating that we change pediatricians. I went, regretfully, to his doctor to ask for his file. Before dropping it off at the new office, I skimmed through its pages. My heart leaped at the sight of each growth chart, developmental test, and record of immunization. (*My baby got his Hib vaccine! He is so clever!*) At the bottom of one page of the file, after routine notes on Theo's four- or six-month checkup, the doctor had written, perhaps with a wry smile on his face, "*Mother thinks child is extraordinary.*"

I did. And I still do.

With our (extraordinary) firstborn safely ensconced in our white ranch house, I knew that I had time—three years, in fact— to figure out who I was as a mother. I would start using my brain again, once I had weaned the baby and I had more time on my hands. Maybe I would return to writing fiction. Perhaps now that I was a mother, I would find my characters richer, more real, more complex. After all, I was a different person than I had been before. I had ushered a human being into this world.

When Theo was only a few months old, however, I learned

that I was pregnant again. It took me about a minute to go from "But I'm still nursing him!" and "But wait! We were supposed to space our children three years apart!" to pure joy. This child was another gift to us. An embarrassment of riches. How fun it would be to have almost-twins. I could see them sitting side by side in a double stroller, wearing matching clothes and finishing each other's sentences into old age. I could not wait until I was far enough along in the pregnancy to find out the new baby's gender.

I wondered whether this pregnancy was God's way of confirming that I was in just the right place in my life. It calmed the identity crisis that had been gusting around inside me for the past year. True, I no longer had a business card or reason to travel overseas, but I was a mother. I would be the mother of two!

Then, when I was about twelve weeks pregnant, I miscarried. Before the cramping and bleeding began, I felt like I was coming down with the flu. I felt off kilter, a bit bloated and not myself. Then there came the point when I knew I was losing the baby. Like being widowed, getting cancer, or other heartbreaks no one chooses, having a miscarriage grants you instant admission into a secret club, a club whose members would rather not be a part of it.

I am not sure why it is so difficult to talk about miscarriage when it occurs so frequently. Statistics indicate that somewhere between 10 and 25 percent of all clinically recognized pregnancies end in miscarriage. Most miscarriages occur, as mine did, during the first thirteen weeks of pregnancy.

There are many layers to the experience. It is marked by pain and bleeding, of course. There are careful medical examinations. Afterward a cloud of fear often lingers. Has some tissue remained that might become toxic? Women ask ourselves, *What*

*am I supposed to learn from this? Will my child ever have a sib-
ling? Is there something wrong with me? Why would God allow this
pregnancy to occur, only to take it away?* The abrupt hormonal
changes in our bodies after miscarriage leave us scrambling to
regain emotional equilibrium.

On top of all that, there is a hailstorm of well-intended, but
upsetting, condolences:

"You can always try again!"

"Clearly there must have been something wrong with the
baby. That's why the body flushed it. You're fortunate you didn't
have it."

"Well, it's all part of God's perfect plan."

"Did you actually see the baby when it came out?"

I recommend saying a simple "I'm sorry."

The doctor who spoke to me by phone when the bleeding
became heavy and later examined me in his office said I needed
to acknowledge that I had experienced a real loss. "Once a woman
is pregnant, she begins to picture her child and how the baby will
add to the family. Will it be a girl or a boy? What will she be like?
You become invested in the idea of the baby. You begin to have
expectations about the child." He was Fred Rogers–like in his
gentleness, and I think I spied a powder blue cardigan under his
lab coat. He told me to wait six months before trying to become
pregnant again and, with a gentle squeeze of my elbow, sent me
on my way.

Because there was some concern that I hadn't "passed" the
whole pregnancy, I needed to go to the hospital for blood tests
the next few days to make certain that my pregnancy hormones
were decreasing the way they should. If my levels remained high,
my doctor said, I would have to schedule dilation and curettage,

or a D&C. In a D&C, a doctor opens up the cervix and scrapes the walls of the uterus to remove its contents.

The idea horrified me.

Please God. Don't let there be anything left. Help my blood tests to come back the way they should, I prayed on the short drive to the hospital every day.

Having to keep these appointments seemed like a mean trick. Instead of picturing the streets lined with well-wishers celebrating the baby I had birthed, these next trips to the hospital were to confirm that I was not holding any remnants of life inside of me. I pushed the stroller into the hospital and followed the hallway to the lab every day that week, glad that Theo did not know about the sibling he had lost. In the end, I learned that a D&C wouldn't be necessary. I breathed out a long, grateful sigh.

In the days that followed, my husband tried to encourage me. "If we can't have more, we can adopt," he said. He knew the idea was not a second-best option to me. I have always believed that God shapes families together through birth, adoption, marriage, and friends who grow to be as close as family. There are no runners-up or second-bests. The children who were meant to be mine would come into my life, one way or another.

I knew it.

I bought a Celtic cross to hang on the wall of my house in memory of the pregnancy that ended. Since then, when a friend miscarries, I encourage her to find something—a rose bush, a cross, or even a stone—to commemorate it. It needs to be her choice and something that holds meaning for her. The purpose of choosing something to remind her is not to hang on to the pain but to acknowledge that something was lost. The cross had special meaning for me not only because of my love of all things

Celtic but because the circle pattern is a sign of God's endless love. Even in my grief and questioning, I held tightly to what I believed to be true—that God did love me, even when I was in pain like this. God knew who my children would be, and in time my heart would heal.

I didn't feel God's presence, but I chose to believe God was with me. It wasn't the first time that was true, nor was it the last. I once heard a priest say, "That's why it's called faith. You don't see it on this side, but you decide to believe. It's not a feeling, but an action, a choice."

After the miscarriage, I longed to be pregnant again. I wanted to feel a baby kick and turn inside of me. I wanted to know that I was the vessel for another person coming into history. I threw the doctor's orders to wait six months and that birth-spacing theory out the window and followed my heart (and my swirling hormones). We conceived the following month.

God indeed had something superb in store for me. Someone, I should say. That June I gave birth to a baby boy whose merry eyes and resilient spirit called for a Scottish name. We named him Ian. Two and a half years after moving out of our apartment on Sterling Place in Brooklyn, David and I were the parents of two young sons.

● ● ●

When we lived in New York City, David and I made a friendship with another married couple that, over the past nearly twenty years, has taken root and grown into a vital part of our family's life. Mark and Mary are more than our friends; they are our chosen family. We met when David and I were considering a move to New York after graduate school. When our former professor and dear friend Jim learned that we were planning a trip to New York, he told us to call some friends of his. He said they had a great place in Chelsea on 22ndStreet and plenty of space to host us. We would love them, Jim promised, and they might just turn out to be our best friends. (Does your heart drop, as mine does, when someone promises you are going to *love* his friend? It just never seems to work.)

Jim's speaking manner was quick, lively. It was a bit like speaking to Alice's white rabbit. "You've got to meet them. That's all there is to it. Call them right away."

We didn't call.

A few weeks later Jim phoned us again to ask if we had spoken to Mark and Mary about our upcoming trip to New York. After we admitted that we had not, Jim said he would take care of it. "You've gotta meet. Just have to. Seriously, seriously. That's all there is to it," he said. A few days later, we came home to a blinking answering machine. (Remember answering machines?)

An unfamiliar voice said, "Jim called and said you are coming to the city and need a place to stay. Please stay with us. We'd love to meet you." Mark sounded like an obedient son, which, in fact, he is. Our friend Jim called to confirm that we had received the message and to make sure the plans were set.

"Yes, yes. We are staying there," we assured him.

We dreaded—as scrappy graduate students who had only made short visits to Manhattan in the past—showing up on the doorstep of longtime New Yorkers who were entrenched in successful acting careers. "Another hundred people just got off of the train," I imagined them singing, their voices dripping with sarcasm, quoting the song about newbies arriving in New York City from the Broadway musical *Company*.

David and I decided that we would be the most unobtrusive guests in human history. We would stay in their home but sneak in and out of the first-floor guest room in such a way that they might wonder if we had ever been there. We would not eat their food or leave toothbrushes on the side of the sink. We would not let the door slam. If we used so much as a fork, we would wash and dry it and slide it noiselessly into the cutlery drawer before leaving the kitchen.

Our second afternoon in New York, after managing to avoid Mark and Mary and slipping in and out of the house with the key they left for us, we heard someone coming down the steep steps into the foyer just as we had walked in. *Should we turn and run?* I wondered. It was too late to hide; they had seen us and stopped to talk from a few steps above us. They were dressed for the evening, stylish and put together. I felt like we were the country cousins in our shabby jean jackets and sneakers. We made polite introductions and then stood awkwardly in the hall.

"I'm sorry. I know Jim made you invite us to stay," I said. I was beyond sorry; I was truly mortified.

"That's okay. It was important to him that we meet," Mark said. He then imitated our friend's rapid-fire speech pattern, his verbal quirks, and the nicknames Jim was forever showering on his friends. "And anyway, we had to meet the famous Dave-a-wave-a-lave and his wife."

We all laughed, connected by mutual love for our friend.

Then Mary told us that Mark was leaving for the theater. He had a show that night. Would we like to come along with her to see it? I don't remember what our plans had been. We might have been planning to pick up some cheap Chinese food, walk to the Imagine Circle in Central Park's Strawberry Fields, and picnic there before tiptoeing back into the brownstone in Chelsea. Instead, we made new friends who would, serendipitously, journey closely with us through the next decades of our lives.

That night Mark gave a delightful performance of Orsino in Shakespeare's *Twelfth Night*: "If music be the food of love, play on." After the show, we walked back to their home and climbed out the first-floor window into the garden behind their house where we drank Mexican beer, ate chips and salsa, and talked late into the night. I remember feeling like a grown-up sitting out there, the sounds of sirens and car horns and New York all around us. Like us, Mark and Mary were people of faith. They were deeply committed to each other in marriage. We had attended the same schools and, in addition to Jim, had other mutual teachers and friends. We spoke the same language, and the same things made us laugh. (They still do.)

Years later, at about the same time David was having panic attacks and a strong urge to change careers, Mark decided to make a change too. He accepted a job in the town to which we would return a few months later. Our lives dovetailed again. As Mark began his first semester as a theater teacher and director, we moved into our first house. The ranch house we bought and Mark and Mary's house were just blocks apart.

That first year back, while my pregnant belly grew and I went to my first doctor's visits, Mark and Mary were trying to conceive. I fantasized that she and I would be pregnant at the same time. We would waddle around town, feel each other's baby kick, and maybe even end up in the hospital at the same time, our husbands running back and forth across the hall, doors swinging open and closed like we were all in a farce.

But this was not meant to be.

●　●　●

A few months ago on a Sunday morning, I surprised my children by saying that, although we were going to church, we didn't have to leave as early as usual and they could wear whatever they wanted. Sweatpants? Jeans? Sneakers? T-shirts? Yep, whatever they liked. We were going to a different church that day. As life-long Episcopalians, my children are accustomed to dressing up a bit on Sunday morning, to following the liturgy, and to the more formal "bells and smells" style of Anglican worship. That particular Sunday, however, we were headed to a high school auditorium where the massive Willow Creek Community Church has a smaller, satellite congregation.

"Uncle Mark and Aunt Mary are speaking at their church," I told the kids. "We need to be there to support them." I half-feared, as I told Mark and Mary later that day at lunch, that when my children experienced Willow Creek's relaxed, contemporary style of worship, they would never again willingly return to ours. When I saw a friendly, goateed greeter hand my children cups of hot chocolate and heard him assure them that they could indeed bring drinks into the service, I was even more nervous. On walking into the auditorium and seeing the massive drum set and electric guitars on the stage, I figured it was all over. Would they ever again darken the doors of our old, Gothic church, with its pipe organ and choir loft, our robed clergy, and the hard wooden pews and padded kneelers?

My children, however, seem to be creatures of habit as far as worship styles are concerned. Although they loved the sermon that was broadcast on a huge screen during the service, they missed following the service in the Book of Common Prayer. They weren't sure what to make of the rock band or the song lyrics projected onto the wall. At Willow that morning, they stood immobile, strangers in a foreign land, as the people around them sang and raised their hands to God in praise.

I would have more fully enjoyed watching my kids experience this culture shock had my gaze not been locked on my friends, sitting in the front row of the auditorium, waiting for their turn to speak. I knew that the story they were waiting to share was the most vulnerable one they had to tell.

When it was time, Mark and Mary climbed on the stage and sat on high stools while a short video played behind them. It was the story of their professional lives in New York and the agonizing pain of infertility. It detailed their move to the Midwest for Mark's new job as a theater professor. It revealed the heartbreak following the rounds of IVF Mary endured. Time after time, they learned that Mary was not pregnant. As I watched the video, my mind flashed to that season in our lives, years before, when I had to tell Mary that—once again—I was pregnant.

We were sitting on her couch, looking out at Theo who was playing in her front yard with a few older neighborhood kids. As we chatted about the play Mark was directing and their upcoming travel plans, I was distracted. I knew I needed to give her the news.

"So tell me all about you," Mary said. She looked tired. The injections and disappointment were wearing her out.

I spoke the words slowly. "Mary. I'm pregnant."

"Oh honey!" She leaned toward me and hugged me close. "I

am *so* happy." The remarkable thing about my friend is that, despite what she was going through, she truly was full of joy at the thought that David and I would have another baby. I had a strong sense that Mary would be a mother someday and wished we could fast-forward in time to that happy ending. It was excruciating to wait.

As I was getting ready to leave Mary that day, I hated to imagine what thoughts would bounce around in her head after we'd gone. When I got home, I had macaroni and cheese to make. I had a mess of watercolors and stray Cheerios to clean up from the dining room table. I had trains to set on their tracks. I knew these kinds of tasks were just what Mary longed to fill her days with at this point in life; she longed to be a mom.

I remembered something a woman from her block had said to us. A few weeks before, this neighbor had stopped to talk as Mary and I sat on her front steps. The woman's mother had recently died after a terrible battle with cancer.

"But you know what my mom told me?" she asked. "She said that the measure of God's love for us isn't how well our lives are going or how happy or comfortable we are. The measure of God's love is what Jesus did for us on the cross."

As I clicked Theo into his car seat, I called out to Mary on the curb. "Remember what Sue said? About the true measure of God's love?"

"I know. I know it's true," she said, and then she turned and went back into her quiet house.

About thirteen years later, on that Sunday morning as my children took tiny, cautious sips of hot chocolate from Styrofoam cups, Mark and Mary described their journey to parenthood. The congregation let out a deep, satisfied sigh when images of their three daughters, adopted from China, appeared on the screen.

"I have to tell you," Mary said, her voice shaking. "I now truly *celebrate* my infertility. If it weren't for it, I would never be mother to these girls. I don't even want to imagine life without each of them. They are the most precious things in the world to me."

In a beautiful, mysterious way, each of Mark and Mary's girls is a specific reflection of—and each a perfect fit with—her parents. One's quiet, wry gift of observation. Another's physicality. Another's tender heart. All of them were chosen, somehow, to be with their parents from the beginning of time.

Although my own journey to adoption wasn't through infertility, I empathize, as much as someone who hasn't experienced it herself can, with those who have suffered in that dark, painful place. Because I haven't gone through it myself, I do not have the right to tell other women to "celebrate their infertility" or that adoption might be the way God will gift them with children.

But what I can say with certainty is that the family Mary and Mark have created together through adoption is not some brave attempt at making up for something that was lost or never achieved. It is not second best. It is, truly, the very best that God could imagine for them. If you visited their house, saw the girls doing cartwheels, giggling with each other, lugging their enormous cats around in their arms, and climbing into their parents' laps, you'd see that these are the people who were meant to be together.

It couldn't get any better than this.

3

Parenting Genius, Dethroned

By the time our second son was born, I had parenting figured out. From anatomy to spirituality to nutrition, I felt prepared to make wise decisions as a parent. I had read everything from Dr. Spock to attachment parenting gurus William and Martha Sears to the What to Expect series. I considered myself an expert at choosing what elements of each of these recommendations and philosophies I should incorporate into my mothering. I was for attachment, yes, but also followed the "get your child to sleep" recommendations of Richard Ferber. After hearing a lengthy interview on National Public Radio with physician and author Robert Coles about the "moral intelligence of children," I let his work guide my parenting choices. I found Carolyn Nystrom's and Ruth Hummel's age-appropriate books for parents about talking to kids about sexuality and their bodies levelheaded and clear.[1] I loved Max Lucado's picture books, particularly *You Are Special*, which I read as much for myself as for my children.[2] If my children could see themselves as the cherished creations of a loving God, could they survive, say, being teased in the locker room in middle school, with their self-worth intact? And, by golly, if Dr. Andrew Weil said to get rid of anything in the kitchen that contained trans fats or food coloring, I did it. In fact, I happily weeded out whatever I determined was unhealthy in our home: refined sugar, milk containing growth hormones, and even the television.

Despite my fears that swerving away from the three-year birth spacing plan was a tactical error, my boys seemed wonderful to me. My older son, Theo, was a sort of Christopher Robin. He was curious, polite, and regarded the world with a steady gaze. Even as a newborn, people would tell me that he was "an old soul." I did not know exactly what they meant, but it seemed a true enough description of Theo. We found ourselves calling him "Little Man," in part because of his rationality. He was always so sensible. Before he was two, I mentioned to him gently that I felt he was getting too old for diapers. I explained that older people, such as his father and me, use toilets instead of wandering around with wet or dirty pants. Theo listened carefully and within the week was potty-trained. Once when Theo played too close to the street, I called him to the front porch where I sat with him and explained the repercussions of a car hitting a child. He listened, nodded, and did not do it again.

Ever.

Problem solved.

Why didn't anyone ever tell me parenting was such a breeze?

I concluded, after having such success with Theo, that all kids were like that. Maybe *all* children began their lives as trusting, levelheaded people and it was culture or emotional wounds or—I don't know—toxins in the environment that make some of them so very irritating, contrary, or disobedient. I would observe mothers shouting at their children in the grocery store and think, *If only she'd* talk *to her child and* explain *why buying that sugary cereal isn't a good idea, all would be well. The nutritional facts are right there. Why doesn't she just tell her child how many grams of sugar are in each box?*

I mean, it worked with Theo.

Ah, well. If parenting doesn't do anything else for you, it almost certainly will strip you of your pride. (Can I get an "Amen"?)

Son number two was the color yellow. Sunny and joyful, Ian spent his later infancy and the beginning of toddlerhood whipping himself through our ranch house in a wheeled walker, skimming along the wood floors with a huge grin on his face. His smile was so broad that on several occasions I worried that something had gotten into his eyes and he was squinting in discomfort. On closer examination, however, I saw that it was just the face-breakingly big smile of a happy boy. At regular intervals during his laps around the house, he would slow down the walker and make a quick pit stop in the kitchen. He would point at the cupboard that held the (organic, sweetened with cane sugar) graham crackers and I'd put one into his outstretched hand. Then he would be off and running again, a blur of boy, the mounted toys on the walker rattling.

I noted with some dismay, however, that the "just explain things to children rationally" parenting theory I was so proud of was not working with him. Ian was not naughty, per se, but he engaged in risky behaviors such as jumping on his brother's bed or running too close to the street. When I sat him down for heart-to-heart talks to explain why these were not good ideas, he did not seem interested. He smiled and nodded sometimes, but as soon as the conversation was over, he was off. The next thing I knew, he was gleefully jumping on the bed again or chasing a ball into the street.

Even my "Aren't you getting a bit old for diapers?" speech seemed to go right over his head.

Ian sat politely through my lectures, stroking my hand and smiling that squinty smile, but then he returned to his former behavior. When I told him that I would be forced to take away one of his possessions such as his beloved cowboy boots for a few days if he continued committing a certain crime, he would nod. "Oh. That's okay. You can have them, Mama." Big grin, a hug, and off he went. I paged through my stash of parenting books in search of answers, but none of the descriptions fit Ian. He wasn't strong-willed or defiant.

Truthfully, he just seemed like a happy little kid.

This parenting gig was getting more complicated.

When Ian was ten months old, I learned I was pregnant again. This pregnancy took my husband and me by surprise, catapulted us into our second house, and strong-armed us into buying a minivan. None of the other cars we looked at could fit three car seats in a row.

"Welcome to middle age!" our neighbor shouted from across the street when we brought the minivan home. Wait—when had we become middle aged? Life was whipping by, like the blur of landscape outside your car window as you speed down the highway past farmland, billboards, and crumbling barns.

This pregnancy made me wonder if we would ever have the chance to adopt. Wasn't three children enough? Reckless, even?

I saw the pursed lips and felt the disapproval of some of our friends when we gave them the news. I imagined what they must be thinking: *Three? Really? The problem of overpopulation means nothing to you? So you're just going to trample the environment under your feet with your plastic diapers and juice boxes?*

Daughter Isabel was born forty-five minutes after we arrived at the emergency room, early one January morning. I hoisted myself onto the bed in the mother-baby unit. The nurse, checking to see how dilated I was, calmly told me that we did not need to wait for my doctor to arrive. She had birthed babies many times and I was very close. Meanwhile, my doctor zipped across town, was delayed by a train, and finally, panting, ran into the hospital room. She checked my progress and announced, "Three pushes and she'll be out."

Seconds later, Isabel was born. After the long and complicated births of my boys (resulting in a C-section for Theo and, in Ian's case, a long and protracted wrestling match between baby's head and a forceps-brandishing doctor), my husband and I were stunned. "Take a picture, Dad," my doctor said. The image he captured is our little girl, still attached to me by the umbilical cord, red-faced and screaming her head off.

"Uh-oh," my friend Andrea said when she saw the photograph a few days later. "*This* is going to be interesting."

Theo was three and Ian was one and a half when Isabel was born—and almost from the start, she seemed intent on keeping up with them. She pumped herself on a swing, tied her own shoes, and rode a two-wheeled bike at much younger ages than did her brothers. As a toddler, she sometimes carefully picked up her brothers' LEGO creations, held them high above her head, and then hurled them to the ground. "But, but . . . !" the boys would cry. Needless to say, sitting her down and explaining that "we" honor what other people have made, that the boys cared about their LEGO ships, and that it hurt their feelings when she destroyed them did no good. She simply stared straight ahead and kept her little arms crossed in front of her. When she could talk, she would explain her naughty behavior by saying something along the lines of, "They make me mad."

Mostly, though, Isabel beguiled us with her intelligence and humor. Ever since she was a toddler, she has been able to do spot-on impersonations of everyone from the UPS driver to our ninety-something-year-old neighbor. Isabel somehow incarnates people, mimicking facial expressions and making chit-chat in just the way they do. She makes us all howl with laughter.

Despite raising three little kids who daily confounded the parenting theories I was so happy to have perfected, the idea of adopting a child lingered in me like a song you cannot get out of your head. I felt like someone was missing. After the miscarriage, I could not shake the feeling that my kids were meant to have another sibling. As the fourth and youngest child in my own family, I sometimes felt like I was waiting for our fourth to come home and complete our family picture.

From time to time, I talked to my husband about why adoption was a natural choice for us. I had already oriented my life around the schedules and needs of young children. We liked the way our family was evolving and enjoyed the culture we were creating together. We were in love with Mary and Mark's girls and recognized that adoption was a precious gift. I'd observe other adoptive parents with kids in their laps at a children's program at the library or in restaurants and I'd feel a kind of longing. The children whom I noticed were adopted, of course, were part of transracial families. Such families, it seemed to me, were creating positive cultural change as they brought more diversity to our community, making it look a bit more like the real world.

When we talked about adopting a child, David and I imagined we would adopt internationally. We have both traveled around the world and have witnessed how children in some of its poorest places live. I thought of kids I had seen in Vietnam, begging outside of the souvenir shops. "*Madame! Madame! Madame!*" they would call, tugging on my sleeve or on the hem of my skirt. My husband would return from business trips to India troubled. He would watch clusters of little children on highway medians, begging from people in passing cars. Meanwhile, on the other side of the world, his children went to sleep every night amid mounds of stuffed animals and books, ear buds playing their favorite songs, stomachs full, and drowsy in their beds.

The contrast was humbling and pulled at our consciences—hard.

But David worried about the cost of raising four children. After Theo was born, I found regular freelance writing work and David had a good job, but after spending our twenties in graduate school and choosing acting and nonprofit work in New York, we hadn't exactly built up a huge savings account. When I was pregnant with Theo, David and I started meeting with a financial adviser. On his first visit, he asked us to list our assets. We sat dumbfounded at the dining room table and joked about it later.

"Well, there's the Crock-Pot," I said.

"And we own the lawnmower outright."

All this, of course, begs the question: how could we possibly, as the increasingly flummoxed parents of children aged two, three, and five, start the adoption process?

4

The Red Thread

Chinese folklore uses the image of the red thread to describe destiny. A Chinese proverb says, "An invisible red thread connects those who are destined to meet regardless of time, place or circumstance. The thread may stretch or tangle, but it will never break." Those invisible red threads connect newborn babies to all the people who will be important in their lives and shorten as these people come together.

The belief that God guides our paths is found in many religions, but it sometimes leaves the faithful troubled. How do we reconcile the idea that God has a divine plan with the reality that about half of the world's children are born into poverty? Given that, what are we to make of God's assertion in Jeremiah 29:11 to know "the thoughts that I think toward you . . . thoughts of peace and not of evil, to give you a future and a hope"?

Is there a big, generous God who created us the way Max Lucado's Eli created the Wemmicks in *You Are Special*?[1] Does this God hear us, love us, and want the best for us? If so, why do some people have comfortable lives while others pick through dumps for the scraps of garbage that will feed their children for one more day? What is the "future and hope" God has planned for the 160 million orphans around the world?

I wonder if we could have something to do with it. Has God given a mandate to those of us who are materially blessed to serve the poor? World Vision US president Richard Stearns thinks so. In his book *The Hole in Our Gospel*, he challenges American Christians to take responsibility for the poor. "It is not our fault that people are poor, but it is our responsibility to do something about it. God says that we are guilty if we allow people to remain deprived when we have the means to help them," Stearns wrote.[2]

Is there an invisible red thread that ties me to the world's poorest people?

Faithful practitioners of other major religions believe that the rich must help the poor. Kabbalah is a form of Jewish mysticism recently popularized in the United States by its celebrity devotees. The word *Kabbalah* means "that which is received" or "tradition." Its teachings explore the mysterious relationship between the eternal, invisible God and God's creation. Those who practice Kabbalah wear red, knotted threads around their left wrists as witness to their devotion to that invisible God. They are urged to share in the suffering of the poor.

Buddhists explain tragic, fateful events, as well as serendipitous moments, as stemming from karma, or the effects of a person's actions and intentions in former existences as well as in the present. Compassion toward the poor and serving them creates good karma. Those who practice Sanatana Dharma, which we often call "Hinduism" and Sikhs are compelled to help the poor as well. Islam's holy book, the Qur'an, teaches that those who do not help orphans or feed the hungry will be punished.

Perhaps one way that God engages with humankind is through the compassion we extend to others.

But God seems to do some pulling of those red threads without our help as well. Doesn't it seem that some accidents don't feel very accidental at all? Why is it that culture-shapers such as celebrity talk-show hosts insist that when a person specifically "sends a message to the universe" about a longed-for life partner or job, that desired person or thing seems to appear?

Some things just work out serendipitously. *Serendipitously*: a pretty word that lets us wave away the possibility that these things just might be divinely ordained.

Mother Teresa wrote, "God made the world for the delight of human beings—if we could see His goodness everywhere, His concern for us, His awareness of our needs: the phone call we've waited for, the ride we are offered, the letter in the mail, just the little things He does for us throughout the day. As we remember and notice His love for us, we just begin to fall in love with Him because He is so busy with us—you just can't resist Him. I believe there's no such thing as luck in life, it's God's love, it's His."[3]

So many parents who have adopted a child are surprised to discover a curious similarity between themselves and their new son or daughter. That similarity can feel like another gift, or like icing on the cake. Maybe you and your child share a freak allergic reaction to watermelon. An inexplicable love for opera. An aversion to cats. A passion for thunderstorms. After seeing the first pictures of Mia and me, several friends were astonished: "She has your eyes," they said. Or, "How is it that she has the Grant nose?"

"It just seems like we were meant to be together," many adoptive parents say. "Like we were always intended for each other." Adoptive parents find the red thread proverb helpful in describing the miracle of how their families were created. It's as beautiful and useful a story as any to talk about the intersection of fate, love, friendship, and family.

"Blessed be the tie that binds," the old hymn says.

Divine providence.

The red thread of destiny.

I believe God nudges us toward the people with whom we're meant to share our lives. And, sometimes, I think God uses adoption to rip away the curtain that keeps us blind to poverty and suffering. In finding our children and falling in love with a country far from home, many adoptive parents find a calling to change their lives and serve those whom they have met there. They know that members of their children's first families struggle just to survive; suddenly the crisis of global poverty is personal.

Is that part of the divine plan of adoption? Not only to give permanent, loving families to orphaned children and to answer the prayers of the childless, but to link those who have much with those who do not have enough? To make us all, truly, extended family?

More and more, I think so.

I believe God does pull us toward our children and our friends with long, red threads. My friendship with Mark and Mary is one of the ways my daughter and I were drawn together. Our friend Jim doggedly insisting that we stay with them in New York. Our families, almost simultaneously, deciding to leave New York for the same little Midwestern town. That I was able to share both in the sorrow of their infertility and in the joy of watching their family take shape as they brought their girls home from China, one by one. Were these some of the ways God led me along a path toward adoption and, ultimately, toward my daughter? I think so.

And finally, just so I wasn't able to miss it, something more direct happened. A message was communicated. It came out of nowhere and took me by surprise. My family's life changed course again.

It was a divine whisper, almost too quiet to hear.

5

A Whisper

The event that made me push aside my fears and start the adoption process is difficult to articulate. It felt, though, as indisputable as holding a pregnancy test in my hands, the lines drawn into a tiny plus sign. I knew that a child was on the way. I was sitting a few pews from the front of my church during a baptism. The babies were exquisite, dressed in their lacy, white gowns. The young parents were nervous, each likely wondering whether his or her child would be a crier or would mesmerize the congregation with that kind of otherworldly calm that comes over some babies during their baptisms.

The front of the church was crowded with children, giggling and whispering to one another, including my three. Some very young kids sat cross-legged on the floor and faced the congregation, unaware of the sacrament that was being received just behind them. Others stood on tiptoe and strained against the altar rail in order to get a better look.

The priest read the prayers and, with the congregation, I responded:

Deliver them, O Lord, from the way of sin and death.
Lord, hear our prayer.

Open their hearts to your grace and truth.
Lord, hear our prayer.

Fill them with your holy and life-giving Spirit.
Lord, hear our prayer.

Keep them in the faith and communion of your holy
*   Church.*
Lord, hear our prayer.

Teach them to love others in the power of the Spirit.
Lord, hear our prayer.

Send them into the world in witness to your love.
Lord, hear our prayer.

Bring them to the fullness of your peace and glory.
Lord, hear our prayer.

The candles' flames flickered and the priest blessed the water, saying, "We thank you, Almighty God, for the gift of water. Over it the Holy Spirit moved in the beginning of creation. Through it you led the children of Israel out of their bondage in Egypt to the land of promise . . ."[1]

Then, in this familiar moment, everything seemed to go quiet around me and I heard a voice. It was not a voice exactly, but I knew I was being addressed. It was a message, silent and wordless, yet somehow fixed in words. It entered my mind, in not a whisper exactly, but as a quiet announcement. Spoken slowly and calmly, yet not exactly spoken at all. As the water fell against little foreheads and was gently patted dry with the crisp white linen, I heard it.

You'll be up there again with your baby.

My baby? I responded silently. My children had already been brought as infants to the altar for their baptisms. It is a sacrament; it doesn't happen twice. We had already stood with our friends and our family, a little cluster of those dearest to us, and handed each baby, in almost perfect two-year intervals, over to the priest. We stood, eyes spilling over with tears, as the water poured over their foreheads and they received the sacrament. Isabel's gown, trimmed in eyelet and satin ribbon, still hung in the back of her closet.

You'll be up there again with your baby.

In that moment, a feeling of peace wrapped itself around me and a few things seemed certain and clear. I knew that the baby who would come into our family would not come to us the way our three older children had. This time, I would not mark off the weeks on the calendar or visit the doctor so she could measure my growing belly and listen for the heartbeat. My husband and I would not see the flash of our baby's heart on the ultrasound screen. I would not find myself yet again at the hospital in a flurry of fluorescent lights and medical instruments as my little one came into the world. In fact, I would not be anywhere near her when this baby grew in her first mother's body and made her entrance into human history. This baby would be born to another woman. The pages of this woman's life story would turn and bring her to the heartbreaking moment of choosing to place her child in another person's care. This baby—her baby—would be no less, and no more, my own than my other children were.

On the drive home from church, I told my husband about what had happened to me. He shook his head, probably seeing in his mind, as he often seems to, a slide show comprised of bar graphs illustrating the escalating costs of raising children. Diapers. Organic milk. Music lessons. Braces. College. (Cue sound of old-fashioned cash register: *ching ching!*)

That afternoon, we got the kids settled in front of a movie in the basement (probably *Chitty Chitty Bang Bang*) and sat cross-legged on our bed upstairs. I told him again what I had heard. I knew it was as undeniable as if I were holding a registered letter in my hands. As we spoke, he, too, felt peace wash over him and a clear sense that, yes, there was a baby, right now and somewhere in the world, who would forever be our child.

"But I don't want a newborn," he said. "I can't handle the sleep deprivation. And I don't want to adopt a child someone else would be quick to adopt. I want to find one who is waiting to be adopted. One who may not find a family otherwise."

Two days later, we attended a meeting at a local adoption agency. The twenty or so of us who sat on folding chairs remained anonymous. We were not asked to fill out nametags upon entering the room or to introduce ourselves. We moved past each other quietly, respectfully staying out of one another's way. We all knew that it was everyone's first time, that we were stepping out and taking a risk by just being there, and that each of us was on the verge of making a decision that could radically change the course of his or her life.

A tray of store-bought butter cookies and coffee sat on a card table. Other tables held brochures and forms related to international adoption programs. The long presentation began warmly but soon evolved into a more difficult set of stories about medical issues, attachment problems, and the unpredictability of the adoption process.

They were clearly trying to scare some of us off.

We sat quietly. When I looked over at David, I knew that he was undeterred by the tales of worst-case scenarios. We stood at the end of the presentation, gathered a thick pile of brochures, and went home to relieve our babysitter.

It had begun.

People still ask me, sometimes in a curious tone and sometimes with a ragged edge of anger in their voices, why I did not adopt domestically when so many children here in the United States are in need. My real—and usually unspoken—answer is brief and springs from my belief that Mia is meant to be my daughter: *I did not adopt domestically because my daughter was born in another country.*

For a less mystical-sounding reply, however, I can describe how international travel has shaped my life and that of my husband. I can list possible obstacles to our adopting domestically, such as our ages and the fact that we were already the parents of three young children. I can confess my unfounded fears of opening my heart to a baby whose birthmother would later change her mind or concerns that an older child, after suffering abuse or neglect, might pose a risk to my young children. I know, though, that these are all hurdles we would have overcome if domestic adoption had been what we'd been meant to do. (People encounter such challenges all the time and build beautiful families.)

In the end, however, like many personal and important life decisions (such as where to live, whether to marry, whether to have children, whether to breastfeed, and what career to pursue),

I had to follow my intuition. I'm aware that it is one of the ways God speaks to me. We would adopt internationally. An older baby. A child on a waiting list.

The invisible thread that connected me to my daughter was beginning to shorten.

May 2002

Dear family,

David and I are embarking on an exciting journey and I wanted to let you know about it and to ask for your prayers. We have decided to explore international adoption and have begun the paperwork process. We are open about lots of the elements right now, but we would like to adopt a daughter. Theo, Ian, and Isabel are thrilled, though we do keep telling them that we are in the exploring and praying stage of all of this.

We aren't looking at China—it's quite difficult at this moment to adopt from there. David would like us to consider adoption from India. He is disturbed by the poverty there and all the kids he sees on the street. Also India has a cultural bias against daughters and many baby girls are abandoned.

We are in early stages, but it's possible that if this is what God has for us, we could have another daughter in about a year. We hope our new child, if this all occurs, will be two years younger than Isabel. We'd like the kids to be in the little close clump that they are in, and David's quite happy to skip over the newborn stage.

Love,

Jen

When I told people that we had begun the adoption process, most were delighted. They sent congratulatory cards. They promised to pray that the adoption would go smoothly and that our older children, as well as the new baby, would weather the transition well. Others were more ambivalent or felt compelled to issue dire warnings about adoption. The white-hot anger of adopted adolescents. Unusual behaviors exhibited by children who have experienced extreme neglect. But what they loved to talk about most of all was how adopted kids had "attachment issues." (Oh, the attachment issues!)

The comments came fast and furious:

"Your family is perfect the way it is. Why jinx it?"

"But you won't know what she'll be like."

"What if she has medical problems?"

"Be careful: some agencies pull a bait and switch, you know, and unload unhealthy babies on people."

"What if she's not as smart or as good-looking as your other kids?"

"Could you really ever love a child who wasn't your own?"

"You're not going to get one of a different race, are you?"

"Can't you have any more natural children?"

"Aren't you afraid that your other kids will resent the adopted one?"

"Adopted kids end up hating their parents."

Then there was the kicker, the absolute hands-down champion comment: "You know; it's not like adopting a puppy."

Um, thanks for the tip.

It's true that adopting a child puts a prospective parent into a situation out of her control. But isn't the same true when a woman conceives a baby? Would a doctor guarantee a woman that her baby will be born without incident or unforeseen health issues? Or that the child will carry on only the best traits of his or her parents? That she'll be terrific at algebra or a talented violinist? Or that he'll be respectful and hardworking when he's a teenager and think his parents are the hippest ones in town? (Not likely.)

I remember standing on the playground one afternoon, watching my three kids play. Theo had just gotten out of kindergarten for the day and he and his younger siblings were clambering up and down the ladders and slides. Another mom, whom I had only met once before, came and stood near me. After a few minutes of chitchat, her tone got solemn and she said, "Can I ask you a question?"

Uh-oh, I thought.

"I heard that you're planning to adopt," she said. "But aren't you afraid that the child you adopt will be different from your kids?"

"Different?" I asked. "Well, she'll be born in another country. That's different."

"No, what I mean is, what if she has a different personality or temperament than the others? What if she doesn't fit in?"

I had to laugh. As with most families I know, regardless of whether their kids were adopted, my three older children are completely different from each other. As a baby, Theo's eyes would light up when he saw a baseball. Or a basketball. Or something vaguely round. He still is a sports fanatic, resolutely kicking a soccer ball around the backyard in the off season. When he's mad, he glowers. When he's happy, he often is quiet, his eyes bright. His brother, almost exactly two years younger than Theo—and born to and raised by the same two parents—has a completely different set of interests. He is fascinated by military history, the rough-and-tumble game of lacrosse, and Shakespeare's plays. On the rare occasions when Ian is angry, he gets tied up in knots of frustration and tears. When he's happy? Well, he usually *is* happy, still smiling that squinty smile of his babyhood. And Isabel? She is a constant reader, a social butterfly, and is wild for everything from softball to romantic comedies to owls. When she is angry, she is a summer storm that rattles the sky and then lights it up with a jagged flash of lightning. When she's happy, she beams, sometimes making up arias of the silliest kind. They are siblings by birth but different from each other in terms of their interests, preferences, and the way they deal with intense emotions. I imagined that like the others, my fourth child, too, would be completely and utterly her own person.

I noticed another interesting response to our family's news. Instead of making negative comments about adoption, some people seemed plunged in a swirling eddy of guilt because they had never adopted a child. It still happens. Someone will hear my youngest child's story and start speaking nervously, their voices rising into almost a cheer. "Oh, she's adopted. Wow, isn't that *great?* I *love* adoption. I've thought about adopting. Adopted kids are great!"

I wait until the speaker runs out of steam and then I try to put him or her at ease. "Please know that just because my daughter was adopted, I don't think adoption is for everyone," I say. (I don't even think *parenting* is for everyone, for that matter.)

I have even successfully talked people *out* of starting the adoption process. One woman said to me, "My husband and I don't want any more children. The thought of it makes me want to crawl under the covers. But there are so many orphans, I've been saying to him that maybe we *should* adopt." She went on to say how unpleasant it sounded to both of them to have another child, whether by birth or by adoption. I suggested that instead of adopting a child, she could consider supporting an organization that cares for orphans or works to empower communities economically. She looked so happy and relieved I thought she might hug me or do a backflip.

That's not the only time I've tried to dissuade someone from adopting a child. When people decide to adopt a child only because they feel sorry for poor children, or simply because they feel guilty about the abundance in their lives or just because adoption seems like the only way to respond to God's definition of true religion ("to visit orphans and widows in their trouble," James 1:27), I worry. I fear that when a person adopts a child out of pity, a desire to be nice, or to help the poor, it might be a very, very unfortunate choice for everyone involved.

What orphans need are families who love them. Period. To be adopted into a family and kept at arm's length or seen as a charity project in what should be your own home sounds disastrous to me. And tragic. Once in a while, I learn of people who have an almost missionary zeal about adoption but truly don't seem enthusiastic about loving and parenting a child. It seems they have forgotten that the adoption process is just the prologue. When you become a parent by birth or adoption, you begin a very long journey.

Remember the analogies section of the SAT?

dove: bird = *ziti*: _____
    a) racecar
    b) pasta

    c) dermatological problem

    d) attire

The correct answer is: b) pasta. You know, ziti? Those little pasta tubes, thin as a pencil and about two inches long?

When people seem geared up to complete the marathon adoption process, but don't seem thrilled—or realistic—about living for the rest of their lives in relationship with the actual child who will soon enough be their own, I think of the following analogy:

    wedding: marriage = *adoption*: _____

    a) celebration

    b) cake

    c) family

    d) gardening

The answer here is: c) family. To unpack the analogy a bit, when despite the tens of thousands of dollars spent on wedding preparations, a future bride and her fiancé seem ill-suited at best, one should worry. Maybe the bride is having a blast choosing linens and cutlery and the groom is having fun reconnecting with old friends and planning the honeymoon, but if they seem irritated by or, worse, weary of each other on those rare occasions they have to be in the same room, perhaps marriage isn't the best idea. Are they just in it for the drama of being engaged and planning the wedding? Have they given time to considering the thornier parts of what marriage truly entails? As a twenty-two-year veteran of marriage, I want to say, "Yeah, but don't forget—the real work begins *after* the ceremony. *After* the honeymoon. It begins when you start to make two people into one. And that is no easy feat."

It's the same with parenthood, right? When you give birth to or adopt a child, you are in for the long haul. You must commit to sleepless nights, vulnerability like you've never known, and moments when you can't even wrap your mind around how much you adore your child. There will also be times when your child's selfishness makes you think, *Who is this nasty little person?* and, even worse, times when you can't believe how brittle and small your own heart is. But because you see yourself as your child's parent and you know you were meant to be together, you wade through the hard times and know that the good ones await you. You ask for help. You admit your faults. You stop, breathe deeply, and count to ten. And you know that whether the weather is fair or stormy, you are your child's true parent.

I read once that the best predictor of happiness in families who have adopted children is the parents' certainty that their children are *meant to be theirs.* Such parents are not just trying to be nice. They are not trying to work off a debt of guilt to the world's poor because they drive a Lexus or own a lake house. They are not trying to be faithful to their religion. Sure, one or more of those things may also motivate or encourage them at various points in the process, but guilt and pity are not the primary reasons they want to adopt. No, these parents know, in some deep, spiritual, and authentic sense, that this is the way their family was *meant to be* created.

Some people come to adoption because they grew up in large families, adore children, and cannot get enough kids into the house. (I know big families like that—and some of them welcomed their children by adoption and others the traditional way.) There are people who grew up abroad, identify closely with another culture, and feel, inexplicably, that theirs should be a multicultural family. There are people who are concerned about overpopulation and the world's resources and do not want to burden the planet with another little consumer. Others who adopt are single, male, or past reproductive age. And there are many people who come to adoption after long, soul-crushing encounters with infertility.

What I hope all of these people have in common when they decide to adopt is a desire for a child—a yearning, a growing desire to have someone else in their lives. To raise a child. To crouch on the sidewalk and look at the bugs. To shop for Halloween costumes. To offer lessons about the right way to eat Oreos. To engage in the hard work of teaching children the way they should go. To deal with the inevitable problems and stress that will happen in the life of every family, regardless of how it was created.

In other words, I hope they come to adoption because they want to grow their families, not because they want to save the world. If your desire is to save the world, adoption is quite possibly one of the least effective ways to do it.

I love the phrase that some adoptive parents use to celebrate their child's homecoming: "160 Million Orphans Minus One!" (Or 143 million orphans. Or 180 million orphans. It depends on where a person gets the statistic.) When I find that declaration posted on a blog or see it stamped onto a piece of jewelry, I feel a chill of excitement. That one child who has been welcomed into a family after living as an orphan is indeed of infinite value. He or she is a child of God, a precious creation who is entitled to a family and a future.

Even so, if you look purely at the math, adopting one child isn't the best way to help the world's poor. If you want to improve the health, education, and economic status of vulnerable children, there are far more efficient uses of your resources than spending them on one adoption. The tens of thousands of dollars you would have to spend just to bring your adopted child home could be donated to a humanitarian organization that does good work. Seventy percent of the world's poor are women and their children. Empower them with microloans, education, a farm animal, or job training and you will see whole communities rise up from poverty.

I'm not just making this up; I've seen it myself. This past year, I visited World Vision projects in Zambia. Some of the women I met had joined together as a cooperative association and had received a microloan. The amount of the loan that the twenty or so women received was far less than what David and I have spent from time to time for dinner at a nice restaurant. The women built a tilapia fishery. With their profits, they paid off their loan, expanded their business, built a school, hired teachers, and made sure all the children—including the many orphans in the area— were fed and went to school. To make the world a better place, invest in charitable organizations that equip women in resource-poor settings to succeed. It works.

Adopting a child is about other things. Packing lunches, braiding hair, spending your Saturdays sitting in a camp chair along the sidelines of a soccer field, stopping by multiple drugstores to find the right bag of animal-shaped rubber bands your daughter has asked for. *It's about making family*. I recently read some (long and rather dull) research studies that listed predictors for successful adoptions. As is the case for parents in general, adoptive families who are happiest and most successful seem to be the ones in which parents aren't suffering from depression, have adequate financial resources, and enjoy the encouragement and support of family, friends, and communities such as the ones offered by places of worship.

When I say adoption should be borne of *desire* and not a choice to do good, some people ask, "Who, then, will adopt kids with severe special needs? Adopting a medically fragile child is more like taking on a medical job. Or social work. But it's still a good thing, right?" Yes, caring for children with special needs, kids who are often invisible in our society, is a *very* good thing. After watching friends and family raise children with disabilities, I have seen that it can be an enormous and exhausting task. Take a look at the children waiting for families in our country's foster care system and prepare to have your heart broken. The stories and all of the sweet faces you will find there will shock you. Prepare to feel anger—and maybe even rage—when you think of the people who have physically or emotionally abused these children. Isn't each child of infinite value to God? Wasn't each one "knit together" in his or her mother's womb?

I believe that people who are meant to adopt children with special needs feel their hearts turning somersaults at the thought of it. They enjoy being around people whom others are eager to avoid or ignore. They know what they are committing to and understand that it's a long haul. They wisely set up support systems for themselves. But parenting isn't just a job for them—they itch to spend time with their children. They enjoy finding their kids fun clothes and toys. And, yes, they feel warmth and affection for their children. It's not an easy calling, but they are drawn to it the way we are all drawn to the things we prefer, the people who make us laugh, the colors that most please us. I believe God puts these things in our hearts.

Years ago, some friends of mine adopted a daughter from China. Like my husband and me, they had children by birth when they made the choice to adopt. As much as they tried to talk themselves out of it (too busy, too expensive, too disruptive to their lives), they kept feeling a desire to adopt from China. It seemed that every time my friend turned on the television, she saw Chinese-American girls: on commercials, giving an interview to the local news about winning an art contest, or just walking through a scene in a movie. My friend picked up a magazine at a hair salon and it opened to a story about Chinese adoptions. Waiting in line at Starbucks, women with their daughters (adopted from China, of course) would appear just behind her. More and more, she and her husband felt their hearts fill with love at the thought of adopting from China. Chinese or Chinese-American girls suddenly seemed to them to be the most dear, adorable, appealing kids on the planet—besides, of course, the Caucasian children who were asleep upstairs during their late-night conversations. After a few years of thinking about it, talking to others, and praying that God would give them a shove in the right direction, they decided to begin the adoption process. Some months later, my friend called me. She and her husband had received their referral from China and she wanted me to come over and see the little girl who would be her daughter. "She's so beautiful," my friend said. I couldn't wait. By then I already had a few Chinese girls in my life—including Mark and Mary's daughters.

I knew she would be simply darling.

I arrived to find my friend staring dreamily at the picture of her new daughter, the way I might have looked at pictures of Rick Springfield or Parker Stevenson in *Tiger Beat* magazine when I was about thirteen years old. She handed it to me reluctantly, hating to be apart from it for even a moment. "Isn't she gorgeous?" she asked, not needing an answer. I looked at the picture and, I'm glad to say, managed to conceal my surprise. Yes, she was clearly a beautiful little girl, but my friend's soon-to-be daughter had a significant cleft lip. They hadn't said they were adopting a child with special needs, so that possibility had never entered my mind. "Yes," I agreed. "She is beautiful." My friend grabbed the picture back and was lost again, staring at her girl in adoration.

A few months after they had returned home with their Chinese-born daughter, I stopped by their house. Only the new baby and her father were home. He was standing in front of his daughter's high chair, giving her dinner. I sat on a stool at the kitchen island and we chatted.

"I love her so much," he said. "But I'm really sad about her cleft palate."

He had never indicated anything but deep pleasure and pride in this baby, so his words surprised me. I tried to encourage him.

"But isn't she having her surgery soon?"

"Yes," he said. "We go in next week."

I was confused. "So why . . . ?"

"I hate it that she won't have it anymore. Look how wide her smile is. It won't be like that anymore." He was almost in tears. "She has the cutest smile in the whole world. I can't believe we're changing it."

That was several years ago. Their daughter's lip and palate have been repaired and she no longer has that "disability." She is adorable in a completely conventional way now, but I know her parents must still sometimes miss that big, wide-open smile. Did they feel sorry for her when they saw her cleft lip? Absolutely not. Were they just being nice to adopt a child with special needs? They were not. They simply loved their daughter and followed the desire that was in their hearts.

Here's another story I love to tell.

I recently met Pam Blackburn, a mother and social worker who, like me, has a blended family of children both by birth and by adoption. Two of Pam's children by adoption are daughters in their midtwenties. One of them, Melissa, has cerebral palsy and is paralyzed. The other, Hannah, has Down syndrome and autism. Both sisters are nonverbal; Pam knows that no one will ever be able to grasp completely what they are truly thinking or feeling. But she watches them closely, interprets what she believes they are trying to communicate, talks to them, and cares for their needs.

Pam is a "saint," right?

I double-dog dare you to say that to her.

"If there is anything I would love people to know about people who have adopted kids with special needs it is that we are *not* saints," Pam said. "We aren't perfect. We make mistakes. We get angry and frustrated. We laugh and cry. We have joys and challenges—just like all parents."[2]

Sometimes people remark that her girls are fortunate that she chose them. "I get fired up about this because, first and foremost, *all children are chosen*," Pam said. "Abortion and birth control are our rights; people can choose them. Placing a child for adoption is also a choice. So, in my mind, if you are raising a child, whether she came to you through adoption or birth, that child was *chosen*."

Pam also bristles when people say how fortunate her children are that she adopted them. Strangers don't seem to believe her when Pam says *she* is the lucky one. She considers herself blessed to be their mother and said Melissa has taught her how to love, laugh, and appreciate life.

She does not feel sorry for her daughters; she delights in them.

And what about HIV-infected children? Isn't adopting a child with HIV tantamount to choosing the grief of burying your own child? Nope, not anymore. I spoke to Margaret Fleming about a year ago, after three of her children, all of whom were adopted, had just started kindergarten. While mothers of typical kindergartners fret over whether their kids can count by twos or color within the lines, Margaret had an additional set of concerns. More crucial to Margaret than her kids being able to tie their shoelaces or hold a pencil properly are the results of regular blood draws that track CD4 counts and viral loads. Margaret's kids are HIV positive.

Margaret is the founder of Adoption-Link, Inc., an agency in Oak Park, Illinois, through which she has placed hundreds of children, many who have special needs. It was in 2002, on a visit to meet her now nine-year-old daughter, when her eyes were opened to the crisis of children and HIV. On a visit to Vietnam, Margaret encountered a hospital ward full of children who had tested positive for HIV at birth. "The HIV ward was the hottest and most inaccessible floor of the hospital," Margaret said. "There was an old fan turning, covered in cobwebs. The babies rocked back and forth all day long. They just sat there, never cried, never fussed. There was no music, no sound, and only a few broken plastic rattles."[3]

She said the caregivers held the babies at arm's length, seemingly afraid to bring them close for fear of becoming infected with HIV themselves. On the back of the infants' shirts, written in indelible black marker, was *HIV*.

"It was like *The Scarlet Letter*," Margaret said.[4]

According to a UNICEF report, globally about 370,000 children younger than fifteen years old became infected with HIV in 2007. Most infections occur during birth or through breastfeeding. Many of these children are orphaned when their parents die of AIDS.[5] Margaret said that a high percentage of the children languishing on the HIV ward on that day were not, in fact, HIV positive. "They probably just had the antibodies," she said. Because infants keep their mothers' antibodies in their bodies for more than a year, standard HIV tests given to newborns yield positive results even when children are not infected. HIV-positive babies are said to "serorevert" if subsequent HIV tests are negative; this occurs most of the time.[6]

On returning to the United States from Vietnam, Margaret created an adoption program for children with HIV. "I vowed I would do something to make a dent in this AIDS pandemic," she said.[7] Already the mother of five children by adoption and in the process of adopting one of the children on the ward, Margaret established "Chances by Choice," a program at Adoption-Link that facilitates the adoption of children who are born with HIV. It was the first program of its kind, but now many agencies offer HIV programs.

To date, Chances by Choice has placed close to sixty children with HIV with adoptive families. Prospective parents who want to adopt a child with HIV are usually directed to Adoption-Link's international program; it is very rare that a child in the United

States is infected with HIV. Margaret said Chances by Choice's Haiti program is "going great guns."[8] The agency works with an orphanage outside of Port-au-Prince where many HIV-affected children live.

Adopting a baby who is HIV-infected is not equivalent to adopting a child with a death sentence. With proper nutrition, medication, and love, the child thrives. Some families, such as Margaret's, are very open about the children's HIV status. Others alert teachers or caregivers but do not make it generally known. Children on strong antiretroviral medications have such low viral loads that although parents should take precautions like wearing rubber gloves when cleaning a cut, the fragile virus is very, very unlikely to infect anyone else.

Margaret's children with HIV are responding well to a regimen of antiretroviral medications. "They take their medications twice a day. I say, 'Who wants to go first?'" Margaret said. She said that one of the medications tastes like gasoline, but following it with a spoonful of something sweet, such as chocolate pudding, eases the aftertaste. "We grind up the pills and call it the magic dust."[9] To manage their HIV, the children also have blood draws every three months to determine their viral load and to get a CD4 count to discern the strength of their immune systems.

The children are living normal, healthy lives, zipping around their house with doll strollers and making Batman toys fly through the air. Their mother is concerned about the long-term toxic effects of strong medications on her children's livers, but she says, "Many people don't understand that there are all kinds of medicines now and if people adhere to the regime, they'll be fine." Margaret admits she doesn't know what course her HIV-infected children's health will take. "We do a lot outside, have a lot of fun. We can't know what's going to happen. We can just love them."[10]

To live in the moment, to celebrate my children in all of their complexity, and to live by faith are all goals of mine. And I learn something about what it looks like to accomplish them when I look at people like Pam and Margaret, women who delight in their kids with special needs. While sometimes those of us whose children are "typically developing" hang expectations on them the way some people put great clumps of tinsel on a Christmas tree, obscuring its real beauty, parents of kids with special needs seem more ready to stop and look at their kids and appreciate their unique gifts. They are in the habit of waiting and listening to their children, while, too frequently, the rest of us fail to look up from our laptops or cell phones when our "typical" kids are trying to tell us something. Parents of kids with special needs do not bother rushing out of the dolphin show at the zoo the moment it ends so that their kids will be first in line to see the polar bears. Instead, they let the amphitheater clear and spend a few minutes talking with their children about what they just saw. While we sometimes wish away our children's childhoods, longing for the house to be quiet and for the children to be grown (only to suffer from debilitating cases of empty-nest syndrome when they are finally gone), parents of kids who are HIV-infected or have other medical issues seem to take each day as the gift it is.

I'm not saying such parents are perfect or somehow super-human; I'm just saying when I stop and look, I learn valuable lessons from them. My friend Mark once said to me that he thought people who have chosen to adopt children with special needs know something about the heart of Jesus that he doesn't know.

"Before you have things like that in your life, you pray, 'Dear God, spare me from that, keep me from having to go down that road,'" he said. "But maybe people who choose to adopt children with special needs know more about what Jesus cares about than the rest of us do."

They certainly see their children more like I think God does.

Part Two
Waiting for Mia

6

Where in the World Would We Find Her?

I expected that the country of my daughter's birth would be transformed from just another patch of color on the globe, speckled with unfamiliar city names, to a place of significance to me. My family would begin to identify with it—we would have roots there. I twirled the globe and saw the countries spin past. *India. China. Russia. Haiti. Sudan.* A slideshow of images clicked away in my mind as I strained to imagine the child whom I did not yet know.

Before being matched with a child, however, we had to complete the home study. There were documents to retrieve from the county clerk and from the dusty recesses of our basement. We completed stacks of forms, got them notarized by our new best friend at the bank, duplicated them, and slid them carefully into express mail envelopes. We met with our social worker. We read books, talked with adoptive parents, and got our fingerprints taken multiple times in ink . . . and then digitally. Our pediatrician signed forms indicating that our older children were healthy. We had thorough physicals so that foreign adoption offices that wanted to check out our BMI scores or other indicators of health would have ready access to them. After several weeks, we were certified by our state as foster parents, but the adoption process had only just begun.

It's hard to miss the irony that while prospective parents by adoption lay bare the most intimate details of their lives, no one regulates who can parent a child who comes into the family the traditional way. Waiting adoptive parents look at the paperwork that is spreading itself over their dining room tables like creeping Charlie, documents that disclose their assets, reveal how good they are to their friends, and enumerate how often they floss their teeth, and think, *Wait a minute. If I were pregnant, no one would get into my business like this. This is just plain unfair.* (Okay, I was kidding about the flossing. Fortunately for me, being a good flosser is not a prerequisite for adoption.)

In the thick of the paper-gathering stage, however, I comforted myself that this expensive and tedious process likely weeds out people who come to adoption for the wrong reasons and aren't ready for parenthood. If you can't deal with the time and frustration it takes to collect birth certificates and financial statements, how are you going to raise a child?

I soldiered on.

Meanwhile, my three children grew increasingly curious. Three-year-old Ian would often ask me how we would find her. "Where is my baby sister?" he would ask.

"I don't know where she is, but God does," I answered. "We'll just take it step by step."

This kind of talk was utter nonsense to Ian. Here was his

mother, serenely pouring half-and-half into her coffee, saying that although he had a *sister* he had never met, we didn't know where in the *whole wide world she was*. He wasn't even allowed to go off by himself at the park and this so-called sister of his got to play hide-and-seek on a global scale?

At about that time in his life, Ian decided he was a big fan of hide-and-seek. He even played it when we were out on errands. After a few minor scares when I thought I'd lost him, I sat him down for one of our little chats. I told him "we" don't play hide-and-seek at stores. I said he must respond to me when I called his name. He smiled and nodded, but at three years old, he must have assumed that I was simply unclear on the concept of the game. He would later admit that of course he heard me calling for him. He had even seen me push the stroller past, with a thrilled little Isabel who enjoyed making laps around department stores at such high speeds. But, Ian explained patiently, it was my job to *find* him, not to *call* for him.

The very last time he played hide-and-seek at a department store, the manager called a Code White and employees locked all the doors. My mind flashed on some predator working quickly in the back of the stockroom, dying Ian's hair in the janitor's sink and changing his clothes so he could steal him away to a salmon-fishing boat in Alaska.

At that point, I hadn't done any research on kidnapping statistics. I didn't yet know how rarely stranger abductions occur. Just one abducted child is, of course, far too many, but my worry as a new mom was disproportionate to the reality. I kept getting the message that almost all adults were out to hurt my children. What happened to those sweet grown-ups of yesteryear with their pocketfuls of butterscotch candies and stories about walking ten miles to school in the snow? Now it seemed like there was an epidemic of creepy marauders who loitered around school playgrounds waiting to snatch a child away.

Every other week or so, I received mail from companies selling teddy bears armed with hidden cameras so I could catch the babysitter neglecting or abusing my child. Or self-defense videos for my preschoolers so they would be prepared to defend themselves from the attack of a malicious teacher or crossing guard. There were ads for identification kits that came with fingerprinting supplies. There were even mailings from companies advertising microchips that I could have surgically implanted into my children's arms. If someone ever abducted my "chipped" children, they could be located via GPS satellite. The profusion of such safety products made it feel more like *when*, and not *if*, such an event would occur.

Happily, since then, I have come to know (and love) the work of parenting expert Lenore Skenazy. Skenazy jabs a pin into the helium balloon of misplaced anxiety and misleading statistics that often distracts parents in our culture and causes them to become "helicopter parents." Regarding stranger abduction, Skenazy writes, "When the numbers are about fifty kids in a country of 300 million, it's a very random, rare event. It is far more rare, for instance, than dying from a fall off the bed or other furniture. So should we, for safety's sake, all start sleeping on the floor?"[1]

There is no need for parents to live in fear that someone is going to steal or hurt their children. Be wise, yes. Teach them how to be safe, yes. But don't live in a murky, buzzing swamp of worry. Most people do mean well. Most people. Some even keep a few butterscotch candies—perfectly innocent ones that have not been laced with rat poison—in their pockets.

"Children, like chickens, deserve a life outside the cage," Skenazy writes on her blog. "The overprotected life is stunting and stifling, not to mention boring for all concerned."[2]

All to say, no one had abducted Ian that day. He was hiding in a rack of men's winter coats until a store employee spied his little cowboy boots poking out from underneath a parka and pulled him out. Caught, Ian emerged, his face flushed from the ambient heat and his eyes as merry as ever. They called off the Code White and unlocked the doors.

"Ian, didn't you hear us calling?" I said, shaking. "Why didn't you come out?"

"Because," he said in his most patient, teacherly voice. "It's hide. And seek. I hide. You gotta find me."

Out in the car, I leaned my head on the steering wheel and sobbed from relief, from frustration, and from embarrassment. It was a good, long post-traumatic stress cry. He and Isabel watched me from their car seats, their eyes wide. Ian never disappeared in a store again. The Code White episode, however, surely made this whole "missing sister" issue all the more difficult for him to comprehend.

"Where is my little sister? Where in the world?" he asked. When I told him I didn't know, he asked more specific questions. "Who knows where she is?"

When I told him that only God knew where she was, I worried that Ian would think that God was playing some kind of game with us. That God was teasing us, hiding our girl. I tried to explain. "There are many children, all over the world, who do not have families or homes. Some of them live in orphanages, you know, like in *Annie*. Some of them have to take care of themselves. Mommy and Daddy want another child, and this time, we are going to adopt her. It is like being pregnant—you know when a mommy has a baby inside? Except the baby comes out of another mommy's body."

From the look on his face, I could tell I was making things worse. I was pregnant and my baby was in someone else's body? How preposterous! What would I think of next? I knew it would be easier for him after we received a referral of a specific child, but first our home study had to be completed.

Our social worker asked my husband and me to write short narratives explaining why we wished to adopt a child. "Give us a sense of who you are. Autobiographical details are helpful," he suggested. David, as ever, was straightforward and to the point. He said we wanted more children. We had a lot to share. We knew there were many orphaned children in the world. We had several friends who had adopted their children. He said, in conclusion, that we were at least reasonably good parents and had the means to support another child, so it made sense for us to adopt.

Done!

I wrote something more like a dissertation. Now that I look back at it, and at the truncated, seven-page version I submitted to our social worker, I realize that I did not write it, primarily, for our agency. In some ways, it was the first letter I ever wrote to my daughter. I began by saying that it was very important to me to create a strong, happy family. I wrote that I thought my new daughter might someday feel alienated or feel out of place because of her adoption. She might grow up with a gnawing sense of being different from those around her. I explained that I would be able to empathize. I had always felt different too.

When I was growing up in a town not unlike *The Andy Griffith Show*'s Mayberry, I had no connection to grandparents, aunts, uncles, or cousins. After my parents' separation and divorce when I was in junior high school, I did not see my father again for more than a decade. At that time, divorce was an anomaly in our town.

As a child, I always felt there was something missing in my life. I wondered what it would feel like to have a father at home. To be taken care of in the way fathers seemed to care for their families. Fixing the water heater. Locking up the house at night. Meeting boyfriends just to make eye contact and let them know that their daughters were cherished and not to be toyed with. Spoiling their daughters and taking what seemed like a special delight in them.

Growing up without a father had troubled me spiritually as well. "God the Father" was often compared to human fathers at church. What is God like? Well, think of your daddy! Would he give you stones if you asked for bread? What was I to make of that metaphor when I did not think my human father had any interest in me whatsoever? Had God left me behind, not unlike *The Great Gatsby's* T. J. Ekleburg, the optometrist who put up a billboard to advertise his practice but then deserted the area, leaving only huge, unseeing eyes? As a child, I had a lingering fear that I would meet my father and he would look right through me. That he wouldn't even recognize me. Maybe my new daughter would have the same kind of fears about her biological mother. What if she had forgotten her? What if someday they met and my daughter's first mother didn't recognize her face?

Growing up, one of my goals was to avoid being pegged as a child from a "broken home." It seemed like teachers and other adults looked down on kids whose parents were divorced. Some of these kids rebelled, acted out, and seemed to be messing up their lives on purpose to show what kind of pain they were in. "He's from a broken home," people would say, tsk-tsking, as though the fact of his parents' divorce explained everything. I was determined to do better, to be an exception.

Maybe my daughter would hear people generalize about "adopted kids." Maybe, as was true for those of us from the broken homes of yesteryear, some people would judge her simply because she was adopted, waiting for her to fail. I would talk about these difficult issues with my daughter someday.

I concluded my "short" autobiography with a look at the role I believed God was playing in our adoption.

I feel God's leading toward having another child and bringing that child into our lives by adoption. I have no doubt that if my husband and I wanted to have another biological child, we could quickly become pregnant. But I want to open up our family in a different way this time. I want to give my daughter a sister, my sons another sibling, and all of us another family member to join in our adventures. David and I both feel that God has blessed us with an amazing family. That I have given my kids the thing I wanted more than anything as a child—a present and loving father—has been a gift to me as well as the children. I see in my own life how God's transformative love can make new life grow from a broken limb. I look forward to embracing our new daughter as she is grafted onto our family tree.

At our next meeting at the agency, David placed his narrative on the desk. "And did you bring yours?" the social worker asked, sliding David's page into a file folder. I pulled my autobiography out of my purse, smoothed the pages, and handed it to him.

He smiled.

"You're the writer, aren't you?" he asked.

"I had a lot to say."

•   •   •

I kept wondering, trying to picture her. Was she Asian? African? Latino? Pictures rushed through my mind. Whoever she was, I was on the brink of forging a relationship with another country, a person of another ethnicity. I laugh at myself when I remember the scattered and incomplete pictures that came to mind when I thought about each of the countries from which we might adopt.

Maybe it would be Russia. To me, Russia is snowy Siberia. Desolate, expansive, and encrusted in ice. It is scenes from *Doctor Zhivago*. Omar Sharif's velvety brown eyes, filled with longing. A plaintive balalaika playing. Russia evokes the smell of fresh dill generously sprinkled over a steaming bowl of borsht. It is the mystery of Anastasia. Bread lines. Gorbachev's birthmark. Tolstoy and Dostoevsky. Priests and icons. Would my little one be forever tied to that massive country that spreads out over the Middle East and Asia like an umbrella?

Or maybe we'd adopt from South Korea. More impressions clicked away in my mind. Chopsticks. Kimchi. The kitschy game show my friends hosted there during the year they taught English in Seoul. When I think of Korea, I think of Eastern religion, Buddhism, and Confucianism. The yin and yang in red and blue on the nation's flag. Respect for elders. Tae Kwon Do. Astrology. South Korea's uneasy truce with its neighbors to the north.

Little as I knew about South Korea, it appealed to me. I knew, after spending time in Vietnam, that there was rich culture and history in the East that I would never know without going there. What was I missing by not truly *knowing* Korea? It seemed like my only exposure to Korea had been *M*A*S*H*, a television show shot in Southern California and not, of course, extremely educational about Korean culture or, really, about that little-known war.

Like so many wars, the war between the United States and Korea resulted in an increase in American families adopting internationally. After World War II, families in the United States began adopting European and Japanese war orphans. Wars in Vietnam, Greece, Latin American nations, and in many other places have significantly affected international adoption.

Would my daughter come from a country on which war left a jagged scar?

Our social worker asked us to come to one of our interviews with a short list of the country programs we wished to pursue. My husband put India on the top of his list. Long trips to Pune, Mumbai, Chennai, and Bangalore have shown him, time after time, how many children are in desperate need in that densely populated country. He feels a connection to the land and culture. "Why not?" I said. "After all, I love the food." I jotted "*India*" onto my list in preparation for the meeting. "Oh, and what about Bollywood? And Gandhi? And the music?" As superficial as my knowledge of the country was, I knew I would love to be connected to that place.

I also knew about the many orphaned girls in India. As in

other parts of the world, sons are highly prized there. Sons serve as a sort of insurance policy for parents: they carry on the family name, inherit land, and care for their aging parents. Daughters are often considered burdens to their families. Organizations such as the United Nations estimate that up to a million baby girls are aborted every year in India.[3] Although it is illegal for medical staff to use prenatal technology to determine a baby's sex, it is obvious that pregnant women and their ultrasound technicians ignore that law. India has practiced gender-based infanticide for centuries; tens of millions of girls have been killed as newborns. The proportion of females to males in India is significantly out of balance and its government has begun to speak out against gender-based abortion and infanticide. The only place girls outnumber boys seems to be in the nation's orphanages, where baby girls are brought after being left in public places or in the cribs and cots left outside orphanage walls.

Would our daughter be one of the unwanted girls of India? The thought that our daughter would be cherished as much as her brothers excited me. Adopting her would not stop, of course, what many call "female gendercide" in India, but it would save and empower one little girl. Our girl.

I felt no pressure to choose one country over another; everywhere I looked there was need. I knew our daughter was somewhere out there, and I trusted that we would find her when the time was right.

As David and I read through packets of information, searched online, and talked together about what countries we felt drawn toward, our lists began to shorten. In order to adopt from countries such as Russia and other former Soviet states, we would need to make more than one extended journey. With three young children at home, this requirement did not seem feasible. The US government had halted Vietnam and Cambodia adoptions due to reports of ethical abuses. There were documented incidents of adoption facilitators stealing children from their families in order to provide Westerners with healthy, young babies. Our social worker had seen some of the art I had brought back from Vietnam and knew I felt a connection to that country. "They might open again soon. Do you want to keep them on the list?"

I spent a few days doing online research, trying to get a sense of whether I could adopt from Vietnam and never wonder whether any coercion, bribery, or other abuse had occurred in the process. Of course, there were many legitimate orphans in Vietnam and many ethical adoptions, but the number of red flags and problems made me, reluctantly, take the country off our list. I felt I just could not be sure.

One by one, we crossed Asian countries off our list. China adoptions were stalled due to quotas, a political misunderstanding between the United States and China, and an outbreak of Severe Acute Respiratory Syndrome, or SARS. Some other countries in the region, including South Korea, preferred that adoptive families had only one child or no children at all when they adopted. Farewell, mysterious Korea. The Indian programs with which our agency worked stipulated that prospective adoptive parents have an Indian heritage or, failing that, practiced some form of the Hindu religion. We met neither requirement.

Weeks passed. Increasingly, I felt my heart pulling toward Guatemala. I knew a bit about its history. I had read about the thirty-six-year civil war that had left its already poor indigenous population destitute. I had seen photographs of its volcanoes, rain forests, and the Mayan city Tikal. I knew of Rigoberta Menchú, the native Guatemalan who received the Nobel Peace Prize in 1992. Menchú dedicated her life to promoting the rights of indigenous people in Guatemala. Reading some of her speeches gave me a sense of what the people had endured and how rich was their native culture.

Latin culture, in general, appeals to me—the music, food, and vibrant colors.

Also, Guatemala didn't stipulate that adoptive families must be childless, and extended trips to the country were not required.

By the time our home study was done, we had decided.

Our child would be Guatemalan-born.

● ● ●

I wanted to learn about what the adoption process was like for birthmothers in Guatemala. From the start, I saw that the country was plagued with rumors and with incidents of unethical adoptions. Our agency said it conformed to strict regulations to prevent abuse and trafficking. They acknowledged that there were lawyers and adoption facilitators in the country who did adoptions so quickly they were seen as suspicious, but the birthmothers with whom our agency worked made birth plans similar to those made in the United States.

Birthmothers were photographed with their babies at the DNA testing to establish maternity. They attended interviews with social workers over a period of several months to ensure they were still certain about their decisions to place their babies and to confirm they had not been coerced into doing so. Some of the protections our agency employed were not yet mandated by Guatemalan authorities but prevented abuse.

I asked for examples of these safeguards and received an e-mailed reply.

> All birthmothers are interviewed multiple times with a non-biased person in the room. (Currently, other agencies and consultants conduct random interviews of some birthmothers to check for abuse.) DNA is tested at a US lab for every adoption and the birthmother and baby are photographed together at the DNA test. This photograph confirms, throughout the process, that the woman attending interviews is the child's birthmother.

Some people concluded that because so many children were placed for adoption in the country, *all* Guatemala adoptions were unethical. I couldn't make that leap, although I'm astute enough to know that the kinds of safeguards my agency and others touted didn't guarantee that all birthmothers were truly making free choices. Even if every person involved in our international adoption was of the highest moral caliber, I wondered to what extent poverty itself twisted and deformed the ethics of the situation, coloring it in shades of gray.

Guatemala has one of the highest poverty rates in Latin America. More than 75 percent of the population lives below the poverty line. (In contrast, only about 15 percent of the population in the United States lives in poverty.) About 50 percent of Guatemalan children younger than five years old suffer from chronic malnutrition. Among indigenous people, that number approaches 80 percent. Guatemala also has one of the highest fertility rates in the Western hemisphere. The low rate of contraceptive use stems from the lack of reproductive health education and family planning services in the country as well as widespread Roman Catholic and other religious convictions prohibiting their use.

As I had expected, my heart pulled toward Guatemala. That country to the south of Mexico became a magical place in my mind as soon as I knew I had a child living there. It acquired a depth and vibrancy at odds with its small size. Somewhere on that pinkish patch on my children's globe, a little baby was living, unaware that in time she would be lifted out of the life she knew into a very different one in a land far away.

7

Adoption: A Crime, a Necessary Evil, or a Miracle?

When he was very young, my son Theo seemed connected to God in extraordinary ways. (Remember the pediatrician's note? *Mother thinks child is extraordinary.*) When he was a preschooler, I believe he even heard God's voice. One day at home in our kitchen, I was working at the sink and he stood on a chair next to me playing with his action figures at the counter. They were the usual suspects—a Wayne Gretzky hockey figure, Batman, and one or more of the Rescue Heroes with those oversized biceps and gigantic feet. Theo had this little posse slink up the wooden slats of the drying rack, one by one, and then slide down to the counter.

"Time to get the bad guys," he said, voicing Gretzky. (Gretzky seemed to be the brains of the operation.) The others murmured in agreement and followed him around the back of the faucet or across a spatula that sat on top of a bowl, spanning it like a bridge. That day, in the midst of his play, Theo froze.

His voice full of surprise, he asked, "Mama, who said that?"

I hadn't heard anything and asked him what he meant.

"That man's voice. It was so kind."

The house was quiet, except for the quiet hum of the refrigerator, the clatter of dishes, or the little thud Batman made when he fell to the counter.

"What voice? What did it say?" I asked. I was beginning to feel a little freaked out. (My son was hearing voices?)

"He said, 'I love you,'" Theo said. He got down off of his chair and looked around the corner into the dining room. "He was right here. I heard him."

"Maybe it was an angel," I said, not knowing what to think.

"I think it was God," he said. He looked around the room again and smiled. Then he climbed back up on the chair and starting playing with Gretzky and Batman again.

His quiet acceptance that God had spoken to him—out loud, no less—floored me. That God would drop in just to say, "I love you"? Maybe that kind of trust is what Jesus was thinking of when He said, "If you don't change and become like a child, you will never get into the kingdom of heaven" (Matthew 18:2 CEV).

A few years later, Theo's uncomplicated faith again made me realize how tangled up my own was. A few weeks before Christmas, he handed me a piece of gray, wide-lined paper. In bright blue marker in very neat letters, he had written:

1. Starwars II Figyr
2. Harry Pottr stuff
3. Transformers
4. Lagoes (Bionigouls, Starwars, and Sokre)

5. Litsabre

6. Books

Need a translation? Transformers are toys that look like trucks and then fold out into human-looking figures. (Or should I say "figyrs"?) The "litsabre" is a *Star Wars*–type light saber. "Sokre" = soccer.

Ian appeared beside his brother.

"Do you know what you want for Christmas too?" I asked.

"Yes!" Ian nearly shouted. "What I want for Christmas is for Santa to bring so many horses that our whole backyard is full of them." (This was a request I chose not to forward to the North Pole.)

Isabel was standing nearby.

"What about you, honey?"

Isabel said all she wanted for Christmas was to sing "Happy Birthday" to "Baby Dejuss" on Christmas Day. A wave of maternal—and misguided—pride washed over me. This was my girl. My wise, pure girl. She didn't want material possessions, but simply desired—Little Drummer Boy–like—to sing to Jesus (or "Dejuss," as she called him).

Ian and Isabel then disappeared down into the basement to play. Theo remained, snapping together a toy Nativity set. I glanced over at him and wondered how I could bring him around to his sister's way of thinking.

"You know," I said, nonchalantly. "When I was little, grown-ups were always telling me that the birth of Jesus was the best thing about Christmas."

"Me too," he said, not looking up. *Click, snap, click.*

"That it's not about presents."

"Yep," he said.

As I began planning a pious sermonette to deliver to this boy, I suddenly wondered whether Jesus' birth truly was more exciting to *me* than the happiness of the season. Was I a liar? A fake?

I took a deep breath and started over.

"The Bible says faith is like a little seed," I said. "It takes time to grow. First, you plant it, then you water and care for it, and later it sprouts and grows into a strong plant. It takes time."

Theo then took us on a brief conversational detour during which he imagined how amazing it would be if you could plant seeds and see them pop up instantly as fully grown flowers, trees, or vegetables.

I wish, I thought. *I wish we could plant seeds and see the final result in a moment's time. I wish my little seed of faith were stronger or would just instantly develop into a full-grown, rooted tree.*

Theo continued his work, his head bowed over the card-board stable.

"Look, if you get more excited about Santa coming or about the presents, that's okay. You never have to pretend to feel something you don't feel. Just keep taking care of your faith, like a little plant. And you know, one day you might feel that what is best about Christmas is that Jesus was born."

And maybe I will too, I thought.

Theo looked up from his work and locked eyes with mine. "Mom, that's how I feel already."

A few minutes later, he disappeared down the steps to the basement to play with his brother and sister. Later I looked at the completed Nativity set. He had gotten dolls and PlayMobil people to add to it and the figures stood in a semicircle around the baby in the manger. Some had their arms raised into the air.

The finished scene looked to be the work of a boy who understood a lot more about Christmas than I did.

Theo had been three when our friends Mark and Mary began the China adoption process. We both were surprised the first time we saw the big bulletin board that Mark had hung in their dining room, pounding nails into the rich, burgundy-colored walls. On it dangled neatly lettered note cards reminding them of deadlines and documents needed for their dossier. Pinned along the bottom edge of the bulletin board were pictures of China and notes from friends. Underneath it was a small table where they had stacked FedEx and DHL envelopes. Little did I know that someday I'd create a similar board of my own.

Neither Theo nor I had seen an adoption up close before Mark and Mary initiated theirs. Theo was fascinated with the dining room's new landscape. Before going about his usual business of avoiding their surly black cat or climbing the big tree that grew through their deck out back, Theo would linger there and look intently at the ever taller pile of express envelopes and ever more packed bulletin board. He knew something big was happening.

A few weeks after the bulletin board went up, James 1:27 was read as part of our church service. This Bible verse is familiar to Christians who are adoptive parents. It says, "Pure and undefiled religion before God and the Father is this: to visit orphans and widows in their trouble, and to keep oneself unspotted from the world."

That Sunday afternoon, Theo stood right in front of me as I was walking through the living room. "What's up, honey?" I asked.

"Uncle Mark and Aunt Mary are going to help orphans," he said.

"Yes, they are going to adopt a baby from China," I said.

"Taking care of orphans is what makes God happy. At church, they read that from the Bible," he said.

"Yes, you're right."

The depth of this little boy's faith astonished me. I started to walk away, but he again placed himself in my path.

"Well, if that is the thing that makes God happy, why aren't we adopting a baby too?"

It was a simple question and one that echoed in my mind for years to come, settled itself in me, and—while I pinned notes and reminders to my adoption bulletin board—I felt a kind of wonder about it. Was I somehow part of something that made God happy?

● ● ●

If you're like me, you never tire of reading stories of how families came together by adoption. You skim blogs written by adoptive parents and you find yourself in tears when, finally, you come to the part of the story when the wait is over and the parents are united with their new son or daughter. Those first pictures of a family, all together for the first time, are priceless. But even though I willingly confess that I'm a pushover for such stories, I'm not an adoption zealot.

Some people believe that adoption is a moral imperative, especially for people of faith. Christians who hold this view cite James 1:27 or the gospel of Matthew where Jesus says that if you meet the needs of someone who is sick, friendless, hungry, or imprisoned you have truly eased His own suffering (Matthew 25:31–46). Could it be true that Jesus is so present with those who are hurting that He *literally* experiences the hunger, thirst, and loneliness they feel?

Not everyone, of course, shares the view that adoption eases Christ's suffering or that it is even a respectable thing to do. The United Nations Children's Fund (UNICEF), for instance, is tepid at best in its attitude toward international adoption and is quite vocal[1] about its potential dangers. UNICEF has warned that international adoption can become an industry in some countries "where profit, rather than the best interests of children, takes centre stage." To help to prevent abuses such as coercion, bribery, or the abduction of children, UNICEF urges countries involved in international adoption to ratify the Hague Convention on Intercountry Adoption.

For some adoptive parents, the fact that *Hague* and *plague* rhyme is more than a phonological coincidence. Although they might wholeheartedly support efforts to prevent unethical adoptions, such parents point out that when a country begins the process to conform to Hague-mandated regulations, orphaned children who might have been adopted into loving families suffer. In better-case scenarios, these children languish in institutions. Others end up on the street, or worse. Some adoptions have been halted midway through the process as countries work to meet the Hague guidelines. Families who have accepted referrals watch, helplessly, year by year as the children they have opened their hearts to grow older, missing out on the attention, interventions, and love they so desperately need.

I understand UNICEF's concerns as well as its goal to improve communities around the world over the long term. Its mission isn't to promote adoption but to protect children from abuse, to better children's lives within their native cultures, and to address poverty and injustice. But can't we give the orphans with whom we share this little moment in history the families and futures they deserve *and* support programs that eliminate poverty? Can't we do both?

I wish it weren't the case, but I think our world will always be imperfect. Wars will tear countries apart and leave those who are most vulnerable suffering and at risk. Natural disasters will destroy cities and leave children orphaned. Death and disease will claim the lives of caretakers. And some women, regardless of circumstance, will know that they cannot care for the babies to whom they have given birth. Even just for those reasons, we cannot justify ignoring the pandemic of orphaned children by saying that we're working on long-term solutions to poverty and injustice such as microloan programs or health initiatives.

Given the shocking number of orphans—whether they are "double orphans" or children whose living parents do not or can not care for them—does it surprise you that some people believe that *all* adoptions are criminal? Whether a child is an abandoned baby girl in India, an orphan in Ethiopia whose parents died of AIDS, or an infant who has been relinquished anywhere from the Glendale neighborhood of Indianapolis to the highlands of Guatemala, they say that adoption is wrong. It might be hard to understand this view in a world of 160 million orphans and in a country where more than 115,000 "adoptable" children wait in foster care for families.[2]

Some such activists primly note that if everyone used birth control or, failing that, terminated unwanted pregnancies, there would be no need for adoption. This argument fails, of course, to address issues such as sexual violence against women, the many parts of the world in which women do not have access to reproductive health services, or the fact that—for a variety of reasons—not all women consider abortion an ethical choice.

Other critics maintain that adoption is immoral because it is bad for the children who lose connection to their birth families. They say people who were adopted are more likely to abuse drugs, suffer from depression, and are less emotionally stable than are their counterparts. I have found a number of these reports to be shoddily designed. Want to prove that kids who were adopted are messed up? It's easy: compare children who were adopted after suffering abuse, neglect, and/or the in utero effects of their birthmothers' drug or alcohol use with healthy children who were born into and raised by functional families. You bet the adopted children will come out badly. (To read legitimate research studies, check out organizations such as the Evan B. Donaldson Adoption Institute and the Dave Thomas Foundation for Adoption. Both are listed in the resources section at the end of this book.)

I don't want to be someone who refuses to listen to critics of adoption while blithely skipping along and saying that "adoption makes God happy." I do not want to be left speechless if someone approaches my family and shares opinions different from my own. I don't want to ignore those who are deeply hurt and offended by my choices. Most of the time, I empathize with anti-adoption activists. Many of them are people who have been injured by unethical adoptions. Perhaps they were once pregnant teenagers whose parents forced them to place their infants for adoption and who were told they would forget all about these babies. Of course, they never did. Some lived their whole lives feeling their children's absence as viscerally as do amputees who experience a tingling sensation in the invisible limbs that have been missing from their bodies for decades. Others who speak out against adoption are the children of American women who, in the middle of the twentieth century, made the choice to relinquish babies but were kept from knowing their children's new names or where they went to live. Their children, too, were denied access to information. Secrets and lies shrouded their childhoods. Through twists of fate (or, you know, God's providence), some of these mothers and children have found each other. Sometimes they unite in their hatred of adoption.

Other anti-adoption activists have seen, firsthand, the suffering of women in some of the world's most resource-poor places. They have heard and documented stories of coercion and bribes. They know of instances where the desperation of vulnerable women has been played upon and manipulated in terrible ways so that rich, childless couples may adopt healthy babies. They argue that simply adopting a child and remaining aloof to the political, economic, and other problems that create a situation in which women must relinquish their babies is cruel. (I agree.) Yearning for justice is a very good thing.

As a journalist, accustomed to conducting thorough research, I had examined the problem of fraudulent and unethical adoptions around the world, including in Guatemala. And, yes, there have been horrific abuses. Between 1960 and 1996, during the country's civil war, Guatemalan soldiers stole more than three hundred children and sold them to adoption facilitators either for profit or to punish parents who spoke against the war, or both. The children were adopted by families in the United States, Sweden, Italy, and France who believed they were adopting orphans.[3] Sadly, some of these children were indeed orphans but only after soldiers had killed their parents so that the children could be adopted by foreigners. There are many more recent cases of unethical adoptions in the country as well.

Are all of these instances tragic and indefensible?

Without a doubt, they are.

But I cannot make the leap to saying that some abuse makes all adoptions unethical, even if—as journalist and American Public Media producer Laurie Stern says—"adoption is dicey"[4] and an uneven exchange. That is, someone who is vulnerable (a birthmother, although some people bristle at the use of that term, preferring *natural mother*) relinquishes a baby to someone who is more wealthy and powerful than she is. Laurie Stern is mother, by adoption, to a Guatemalan-born son. After bringing him home to St. Paul, she noted that members of a Latino resource center near her home seemed to be passing judgment on her family instead of welcoming them into the community as she had expected they would. She wondered whether they thought she had engaged in an unethical act in bringing her son out of his native land.

Stern addresses critics of adoption directly and appreciates their concerns. "Adoption is dicey by definition, a transaction between unequals," Stern writes. In her article "Nine Months in Guatemala," she explored the issue further. "It takes money to adopt, and desperation to relinquish a baby," she wrote. "It's an imperfect system in an unfair world."[5]

Who doesn't wish that all babies were born into functional families and had parents who would cherish them, provide for their physical needs, and raise them to be wonderful, creative, compassionate people? Wouldn't it be great if our world were more like Garrison Keillor's fictional Lake Wobegon, where "all the women are strong, all the men are good looking, and all the children are above average" [6]? Sadly, many parts of our communities, nation, and world are nothing like that. If you need a grim reminder of how broken our world is, just take a look at online listings of kids waiting in foster care for adoptive families. Read stories of abuse, drug exposure, and neglect, and you will get a bitter taste of how unfair this world is.

Stern first met her son Diego in 1999. Since then she has spent the equivalent of several years in Guatemala. She has, retroactively, created a sort of open international adoption for her son. He knows his birth family and feels a strong connection to his heritage. Stern and her husband are transparent with Diego about circumstances around his birth and relinquishment. Over the years Stern has spoken to many Guatemalan women who made the choice to place their children for adoption.

Indigenous women often work sixty or more hours a week as maids in Guatemala City, in sweatshops, or on plantations picking coffee or other crops. When these women decide to place their babies for adoption, their desire is to make the best choice possible that they can for their babies and for their children at home. In areas where more than two-thirds of the population is malnourished, birthmothers who choose to place children express their relief at having the option to do so. I recently asked Stern how many of the birthmothers with whom she has spoken over the years feel that they were coerced into relinquishing their babies.

Her answer surprised me.

"None," she said.

I know it's not that simple, as does Laurie Stern. To what extent is poverty itself a form of coercion? I asked Stern for her thoughts. "As someone who wonders, I am compelled to keep asking it as part of the adoption discussion—to remind people that there is another woman at the other end of the equation, or another country, depending on the frame. That's all I really know how to do as a journalist," she said.[7]

Indigenous women in Guatemala lead difficult lives. They are the victims of discrimination. They watch as their native culture crumbles. They barely get by financially. No wonder there is such a high incidence of depression and alcoholism among them. Placing a child for adoption can be the best choice in a difficult situation.

I've heard people speak eloquently, and with great intelligence, about the problem of evil. Do I understand why God allows suffering? (Absolutely not.) Can I efficiently explain why bad things happen to the world's most vulnerable people? (No, again.) Do I think God allowed my child's birth family to be poor so that I could enjoy her as my own? (No, no, no!) In the mystery of faith, however, I do believe God planned for us to be together. Maybe in our case and in many, many others, adoption is a brilliant plan B in an imperfect world.

In the years prior to adopting my Guatemalan-born baby, I wrote about street kids in Latin American countries. I learned about the lives of "glue sniffers" or *resistoleros*, named for a brand of glue that is sniffed by homeless children to provide a high that staves off feelings of fear, pain, cold, and hunger. Long-term sniffing results in brain damage, among other tragedies. Their situation horrified me. Would my daughter have ended up on the streets if my husband and I had not adopted her? I can't even think about it. Do I have any responsibility to those street kids still living in poverty in Guatemala? I believe I do.

I think, along with bringing a child into our family, we also have the responsibility to work for justice for the kids who never are swooped out of suffering and made a part of a family who loves them and gives them a future.

Adoption is a spiritual journey, and it is one that continues to challenge me to look closely at the parts of the world I would rather not know about, places I would rather not see for all the ugliness and sorrow there.

I think about my son Theo who, years before we started the adoption process, asked me a simple question: "Well, if that is the thing that makes God happy, why aren't we adopting a baby too?"

● ● ●

In my mind's eye, I see two pictures, in each, a different young girl.

These girls could never imagine the other's existence or the way their lives would be linked together. The pictures tell a story that began before the two were born and will continue long after they have been distilled in the minds and bodies of their children and grandchildren. The pictures are jumping-off places for a story about how the lives of these two girls intersected, how they were knocked together like flint and a piece of steel, and how they made sparks and lit a fire.

The first is a picture of me at about five years old.

I'm sitting cross-legged on an olive green couch and watching *Sesame Street* in the basement. I'm reciting the alphabet, repeating *"uno, dos, tres,"* and singing *"Tu me gustas,* I like you" along with Maria and Luis. I like Maria and Luis. They are the only Latino people I know and this is the only place I hear the Spanish language spoken. I like to roll Spanish words around in my mouth: *amigo, por favor, muchos gracias,* and *adiós.*

The kids at my school don't look like the kids on *Sesame Street.* We are fair-skinned, and our surnames point directly at northern European ancestry: Andersen, Baumgartner, O'Malley, Smith, Wagner. I will be in junior high before I will be in class with a child of color.

My neighborhood doesn't look like *Sesame Street* either. In mine, every house on the block is different from the next and there is ample space between each one. They are ranches, split-levels, brick colonials. My brother Drew and the boys across the street use metal garbage can lids as shields and play Captain America in the street. I take the neighbor's beagle, Beauregard, for walks around the block. I live in a yellow split-level house right before the road swerves around a corner and becomes a different street altogether.

We have a big willow tree and a log playhouse in the backyard. I drag sticks across the grass and carry them, along with armloads of leaves, into my playhouse. I tear the leaves into tiny pieces and crumble dirt and dry grass together to make a pretend stew. I wear my brown hair in braids and like to imagine I am Laura Ingalls from *Little House on the Prairie*. My doll, her face splattered with mud, sits in the corner of the playhouse waiting for her dinner. She is Laura's little sister, baby Carrie.

There is a creek at the end of the road. I slide down the muddy banks and look for toads. I jump across the shallow water on the flat tops of rocks, and climb up the steep bank on the other side. There are woods on the other side, and after I pass through them, I find myself in endless fields of Queen Anne's lace, clover, and milkweed. It is like traveling to another land, going beyond the trees into the tall grasses. This time in my life is bare feet, jean shorts, a T-shirt with *I'd Like to Teach the World to Sing* printed on the front.

When I am a little older, I walk downtown with my brother

Drew or with friends to buy penny candy from the shops on Front Street. We like Charleston Chews and Now and Laters. We tear open Wacky Packages. We linger in stores when our favorite songs come on the radio. We listen to WLS where Larry Lujack and John Landecker play "If You Like Piña Coladas," "Muh-muh-muh-my Sharona," and "Staying Alive" over and over and over again. At sleepovers, it's Jiffy Pop, A&W root beer, Magic 8 Ball, and *The Dukes of Hazzard*. Or when we are really lucky, *Battle of the Network Stars* is on. (*Is it always a summer afternoon in southern California? And isn't Richard Hatch from* Battlestar Galactica *a hunk?*)

Sometimes my friends and I walk downtown to the movie theater on Hale Street. We sit in the middle of the theater, a long row of girls from school. We eat salty popcorn out of boxes and crane our necks to see who comes in when one of the doors swings wide and the bright sun blasts into the Grand Theater. The Grand has a rich history, but we don't know about it. If someone would mention to us that Buster Keaton once performed on the stage that now is hidden behind the giant movie screen, we would probably say we "couldn't care less." (*Huh? Who's he? What's vaudeville?*)

The Grand was built by John Eberson, who, in the first part of the twentieth century, was famous in theater design. It opened in 1925, and later that year Keaton came to town to perform. He likely scribbled his name on the dressing room walls, leaving behind a part of the priceless graffiti you can still see if you sneak into what is now a dilapidated building and climb the steps behind the stage. Eberson was famous for creating "atmospheric" theaters whose interiors evoked the outdoors. When I was a girl, the domed ceiling of the Grand still had twinkling stars, but during the vaudeville days, while the audience found their seats, lights replicated the effect that the sun was high in the sky. The sun then set and the stars—comprised of nine hundred light bulbs—came out when it was time for the show to begin. Enchanting.

The girl in the second picture is a year older than I am. She hasn't heard of the Midwest, hasn't tasted a Slo-Poke, hasn't watched John Travolta and Olivia Newton-John dance around the bleachers of Rydell High extolling the virtues (and vices) of summer love, and she certainly doesn't need Eberson's nine hundred light bulbs to see a magical night sky. She lives in the central highlands of Guatemala where the stars shine brighter than those light bulbs, right above the mountains.

Her eyes are dark, her skin rich brown, and her hair is black and very thick. She wears it down, loose around her shoulders. She will braid it together with a brightly woven *cinta* when she is older. When she is worried or concentrating, she draws her eyebrows together. Perhaps she wears that expression when she walks out at night and looks up at the sky above her home. Her house is small, constructed with sun-dried bricks and roofed in corrugated metal.

The girl in the photograph likely speaks a Mayan language, *K'iche'*, perhaps. If there is a school nearby, the instruction is in Spanish, but she probably isn't in school much. She's needed at home to care for younger siblings.

The land she lives in is rugged and green. The closest city is Antigua, situated in a valley surrounded by three volcanoes that stand around it like protective uncles. She probably goes into Antigua's *mercado* regularly to buy fresh meat or fruit—mangoes, cherries, and *lychas*. Perhaps her relatives sell handwoven cloth there.

Spanish conquistadors founded present-day Antigua in 1543. Earthquakes, erupting volcanoes, and political conflict have battered the city since then. *Volcán de Fuego*, or volcano of fire, has kept its rage simmering since the Spanish came, issuing smoke almost daily as a sign of its fury. The city rests in the shadow of *Cerro de la Cruz*, or the Hill of the Cross. The volcano and the huge Roman Catholic cross are reminders of the cycles of peace and violence that have defined Guatemala's broken history.

It is not an idyllic time to be living here for the girl and her family. In the hills, just out of sight, are men with machine guns. The country, already bloodstained from outsiders' attempts to take it captive, is now locked in a treacherous civil war.

As a little girl growing up in the Midwest, I had never heard of Guatemala. I thought volcanoes were the stuff of the Paleolithic period. They didn't still exist, right? I mean I'd never seen one in Illinois. And I didn't know what the term *Cold War* meant, even though many of the adults around me surely lived in fear of Russian expansion. Cold War politics would influence America's involvement in Guatemalan affairs. In the mid-1950s, before either of us was born and around the time when Buster Keaton's friend Charlie Chaplin was denied entrance to the United States on suspicion that he was sympathetic to communists, the CIA orchestrated the overthrow of Guatemala's socialist president, Jacobo Arbenz Guzmán. Our nation was concerned that communism would stake a claim in our hemisphere.

The new military regime hurt the indigenous people, people like this girl and her family. They were driven from their land and further into poverty. Hundreds of thousands of Guatemalan people died. Unspeakable atrocities were committed. And the effects of this war certainly played a role in this Mayan girl's decision, about thirty years into the future, to entrust a stranger with the precious gift of her daughter.

•   •   •

There came a point as a new mom when I realized my brain was going to mush, like a jack-o'-lantern that has sat outside on someone's front stoop too long after Halloween. The triangle eyes start to collapse in on themselves. Spots of green mold begin to pop up around the lone carved tooth. The squirrels don't even want to snack on it anymore. I realized the extent of my problem on the way home from Target one afternoon. I had seen an acquaintance in the diaper aisle and as we chatted pleasantly, she did the unthinkable. Between remarks about a toddler basketball program at the community center and plans to meet for coffee someday, she reached over and flung a great maroon megapack of Huggies into her cart. Huggies. My first thought was that, much as I felt a connection to her at the recent cookie exchange, we clearly had nothing in common.

It wasn't that I was opposed to disposable diapers—my problem was that she chose Huggies. What was next? Filling the baby's bottle with Orange Crush? Tossing Lunchables on the couch in the evening so the family could eat dinner while they watched crude sitcoms on television? For reasons I can no longer remember, I had decided that there were two types of people in the world: Pampers People and Huggies People. (And, trust me, you did not want to be in the latter category.) The few times David committed the cardinal sin of bringing Huggies home, I secretly wondered whether I really knew him at all. *Was this marriage just a sham?*

Like many new parents who live in that twilight zone of very little sleep, an upended life and identity, and endless wading through the morass of conflicting *expert* opinions on everything from babies' sleep positions to the right time to introduce rice cereal, I had lost perspective. Driving home from Target that day, while trying to figure out how to extricate myself from the coffee date she and I had just arranged, I lapsed into a moment of temporary sanity.

Who cares what brand of diaper she uses?

Who cares which one I use, for that matter?

What is happening to me?

I knew I needed some adult conversation, stat—and not about indicators for kindergarten readiness or the dangers of high fructose corn syrup.

I decided to start a book club. I submitted a note to the bulletin of my small Episcopal church. The handful of people who responded was just what the doctor ordered. They were mostly male, mostly fifteen to thirty-five years older than me, and mostly off-the-charts intelligent. We represented a variety of opinions about politics, popular culture, and theology. Those who were parents had children who had departed the baby stage. In fact, almost all of them who were parents were already empty-nesters. In other words, this was not a group of people who would enjoy discussing the most recent episode of *Teletubbies*. (They would not be able to define "tubby custard" and hadn't even heard about the recent controversy involving Tinky Winky. *Eh-oh!*)

My favorite new friend in the club was a man who had recently retired from a career in finance. We were very different from each other—and not just because of gender and age. He had a life I couldn't imagine: golf, volunteering, and Early Bird dinners with his wife. I'm sure he couldn't identify with my life as a mom either, with my growing brood of babies and the dried spit-up ever on my shoulder. As a young man, he had served in the military and his taste in literature tended toward battle stories such as Patrick O'Brian's *Master and Commander*. I liked classic literary novels: Henry James, Milan Kundera, and Jane Austen among them.

But somehow we were kindred spirits. The same jokes in the homily made us laugh, and the same ones didn't. At coffee hour or a church picnic, I would gravitate toward him to chat. I noticed that he seemed to be the first person to contribute to our church's outreach projects. When he spoke about people who were, as they say, "less fortunate," there was nothing maudlin or patronizing in his tone. Every week in our liturgy we promise to "respect the dignity" of every person. He was a model to me of what that looks like.

In addition to my Patrick O'Brian–reading friend, there were five or six other regular members of the club. One of the women was a mommy but was just as eager as I was for adult conversation. Laurie would become a dear friend and come valiantly to my rescue midway through my daughter's adoption a few years later. A priest from the church joined book club too. It seemed that he read the flap of the book five minutes before we met every month and then during the course of the evening made sage pronouncements about the book being "a breakthrough work" or "a departure for this acclaimed author." Two of the others regulars were Steve and his wife. Steve worked from home and somehow made a good living predicting trends in the stock market.

At that time in the late 1990s, my husband, David, was newly ensconced in the software industry (post–New York, post–"friends theater"), and it seemed that every few months, he received a promotion and a raise. But, much as things seemed only to be getting better, Steve would issue bleak news. "There's going to be a correction," he said. "I'm not saying it's going to be the Great Depression, but it will be serious. Our debt levels are getting too high. We're overconfident. Trust me, a correction is on its way."

The way he uttered the word *correction* was disturbing. I was beginning to understand how expensive it was to raise children and didn't like hearing him deliver these ominous economic forecasts. I was willing to accept that Steve was a genius. (That's what everyone said of him when he wasn't in the room: "Steve— he's a genius.") But genius or not, his dire predictions didn't seem likely. Everywhere I looked, people were building huge additions onto their homes or installing entertainment systems with surround sound and flat-screen televisions in their family rooms. They were taking vacations to the Mayan Riviera or renting villas in Tuscany. Every year, David received retention bonuses or stock options that we would use to replace the water heater, go on an IKEA shopping spree, or, later, pay adoption costs.

Maybe Steve just had a bad attitude.

At book club, whenever Stock Market Steve started talking about "the markets," I let my mind wander. I grabbed a few more chocolate-covered almonds or scooped a little more artichoke dip onto my plate. I'd glance around the room and try to imagine what the house had looked like before anyone had moved in. I'm one of those former English majors who never took an economics class and sort of sticks her fingers in her ears and says "la la la" when people start using words like *amortization* and *securities*. In college, when I'd meet someone who identified himself as a business major, I felt like I did when that woman put Huggies in her shopping cart.

Who are you? I'd wonder. *Are we even the same species?*

While the "econ" or business majors were learning what makes the global economy go around, I was in a poetry seminar or skipping class and having a long-overdue conversation with a friend about what we'd be like when we were middle-aged or taking the train into Chicago to stare, Ferris Bueller–like, at Georges Seurat's *A Sunday on La Grande Jatte.*

Truth be told, I don't even play Pit when the rest of my family chooses it for game night. *Barley? Soybeans? What?* I make the popcorn, refill the kids' 7-Up, and tidy up the junk drawer instead. As I separate the double-A from the triple-A batteries, my husband and kids slam cards down on the table, laugh wildly, and pound on the bell. It's fun to watch them, but I don't want to play. It's just too math-y for my tastes.

Despite my lack of interest in economics or reading about oceanic battle scenes, I liked my funny little Island of the Misfit Toys book club. It gave me something more important than diapers to think about. It also gave me new friends, ones with lives very different from my usual mommy crowd. The diverse, intergenerational group also gave me insights into different perspectives about the world, replacing some of the judgment in my heart with compassion, some of my pride with humility.

One month, for instance, we read *Snow Falling on Cedars.* The novel, among other things, is about the internment of Japanese-Americans in the United States in the early 1940s after Pearl Harbor. Somehow, despite being pregnant and having an infant and a toddler, I had finished the book. (*Chitty Chitty Bang Bang* very likely came to my rescue.) The story broke my heart and I had come to our meeting that night on the verge of tears and in a cloud of self-righteous anger. Although I knew that Japanese-Americans had been the victims of prejudice after Japan attacked Pearl Harbor and although I remembered learning something about internment camps, until I read David Guterson's book, I had not really fathomed what life was like for Japanese-Americans then. Maybe I had skimmed over that chapter in my history textbook or skipped class the day it was covered. More than 110,000 people forced to leave their homes for communal barracks? The dreadful financial losses, emotional wounds, and even deaths suffered by American citizens? I was horrified.

That night my gentle-hearted, Patrick O'Brian–loving friend told us that *Snow Falling on Cedars* deeply upset him. Reading it, he grieved for the first time for the terrible wrong that had been done to Japanese-Americans. He said what most affected him was facing the truth that when they were confined into the camps, he had been very pleased indeed. During the past month, however, while reading Guterson's novel, he had realized that the support he gave as a younger man for the camps had not been rooted in patriotism or concerns about national security.

"It was racism," he said. "Plain and simple."

He said he always thought of himself as a fair-minded person. Caucasian himself, he had close friends who were African-American and had worked with many people of color throughout his career. He confessed, however, that after Japan's attack on Pearl Harbor, seeing any Asian person was anathema to him. That racism lingered. German or Russian Americans weren't targeted during that time, he noted, the way those with Asian features were. Those with European heritages blended easily into the larger culture and could go about their lives, invisibly.

"It's not an excuse," he said, "but I can't tell you how terrifying Pearl Harbor felt to us. That our own land was attacked
like that. That anyone could come so close. Nothing like that had
ever happened before. When you're scared, sometimes you don't
think clearly. You can lose sight of what is right."

Decades later, he said he felt only indifference when then
President Ronald Reagan signed legislation apologizing to Japanese-
Americans for the "race prejudice, war hysteria, and a failure of
political leadership" that led to the war relocation centers.[8] That old
prejudice was still in my friend, lying dormant. But reading *Snow
Falling on Cedars* broke him open wide and showed him the ugliness of his prejudice. In confessing it, he was able to be rid of it.

Hearing this good man's confession made a deep impression
on me. I would remember the evening's conversation a few years
later, after 9/11, when fear of Arab-Americans seemed rampant.
My sympathy for Arab-Americans spilled over, touching even the
people who were crippled by fear after 9/11 and who lost sight
of right and wrong in their judgment of all people who looked
Middle Eastern to them. Racism is inexcusable, but maybe
acknowledging unspoken fears, disappointment, and grief would
be a good step in ridding ourselves and our culture of it.

I think about that night at the book club, too, when I read
about the CIA replacing Guatemala's president in the 1950s with
a leader of our own choosing. We felt justified ousting the former
president because he was a socialist. Some people in the United
States were afraid he had ties with Russia. The dictator whom
we placed into power revoked the reforms that Guatemala's former president and his predecessor had instituted. These included
agricultural reform that had aided the indigenous people at the
expense of the US-owned United Fruit Company.

Ever wonder what the term *banana republic* means? (No, no, not the clothing store.) It describes an unstable Central American country ruled by a powerful, wealthy minority whose economy depends on limited agriculture, such as bananas. After the coups d'état, the indigenous people were forced to leave their rich farmland and move to smaller plots at higher elevations. Many worked for very low wages on huge United Fruit plantations to support themselves. Conflict between the government and insurgent groups continued until 1996; it was a civil war.

Three years after the civil war ended in Guatemala, the United States released documents that revealed that although we were aware of atrocities committed by the Guatemalan army, our government continued to provide it with training and aid. Children were abducted, sexually abused, and were sometimes forced to become soldiers. Others were buried alive. Women were raped. Fetuses were cut from their mothers' wombs. When these documents became public in 1999, President Bill Clinton traveled to Guatemala and formally apologized on behalf of the United States. That brutal civil war is one of the threads that tie our two countries together. It's an ugly one, but there is no denying that it winds through the beautiful, imperfect tapestry that tells the story of my daughter and me.

Throughout this time, the Mayan girl in Guatemala's highlands grew up. I know the way she furrowed her brow from the one photocopied image I have of her. In it, my daughter's birthmother holds her baby on her lap on the day of a blood test that determined their matching DNA. She wears a stoic look on her face and her forehead is marked with a distinct crease, one that took years to develop. When the picture was taken, she hadn't seen her daughter since the baby was a few days old and was given into the care of a foster mother. On the day of the picture, she knew she was likely seeing her baby for the last time.

Did God orchestrate the civil war? Was God blind to torture? Did God forget the poor in Guatemala? Certainly not, but God did design a plan for the baby daughter whom the Mayan woman would bear. She would be safe from the instability and corruption that continues to plague the land of her birth. She would have enough to eat and would fulfill the dream of her first mother and go to school.

Not only that, but she would be cherished beyond words.

● ● ●

After deciding on Guatemala, our social worker then talked with us about whether we were open to adopting a child with special needs. Would we accept a referral of a child with a small, repairable issue? Club foot? Cleft palate? Lazy eye? What about a child who had been diagnosed with a cognitive, behavioral, or speech problem? Were we prepared to adopt a child with more significant medical problems such as cerebral palsy, fetal alcohol syndrome, or spina bifida? It felt odd, almost surreal to check off some boxes and not others. I knew that if I had been pregnant, I could not have filled in forms indicating whether I was willing to have a child with one type of medical issue over another. In my pregnancies, I had refused amniocentesis testing. I trusted God to give me whatever resources I needed to parent my child. The question of whether we would *choose* to adopt a medically fragile child or one with special needs was trickier to answer.

David had worked with profoundly physically and mentally

disabled people the summer we started dating. He fed and bathed clients. He helped them exercise. He took them on outings to parks and swimming pools. Often clients with whom he was working could not communicate in a traditional way, but David knew they were trying to connect. Sometimes they nodded or squeezed his hand. Sometimes he felt he knew what they were feeling from observing a new twinkle in their eyes. I was amazed by the delight he took in what seemed to be an incredibly physically and emotionally demanding job. The way he spoke about his clients contributed to my falling in love with him. Surely he would be a wonderful parent to a child with special needs.

We prayed that God would continue to guide us toward the child who was meant to join our family. In the end, we decided, given the young ages of our other children, that we would not request a child with special needs. David was still traveling a lot in his work. He went to India for extended trips a few times a year and made frequent domestic business trips. There were regular intervals when I was, effectively, a single mother for a week or two at a time. Accepting a referral of a child with less significant medical issues didn't trouble us, but we felt certain that it wasn't the time to adopt a medically fragile child or one with larger issues. Again, we felt we had to be open and follow our intuition, trusting that God would use it to guide us. We submitted the final forms and awaited the home visit.

I don't know anyone who hasn't panicked on some level about the home visit, a required part of the home study. As soon as I heard about it, I spent my spare time obsessively cleaning my house, scouring every closet, finding mates for every sock, and digging around in the corners of the kitchen cupboards so every storage container had a matching lid. I checked the kids' coat pockets for candy wrappers and little balls of lint. I scrubbed the floors with Murphy Oil Soap.

For the record, however, social workers don't check for cobwebs in the chandelier or dust bunnies under the beds during the home visit. Ours didn't, anyway. And they don't make sure that every outlet is rendered inoperable with a plastic child protector. Our social worker didn't even seem to care that the eggs in our refrigerator were organic and cage-free.

The home visit came and went: we passed. But now that our home study was done and our dossier was complete and sent to Guatemala, who would our child be?

I looked at photos of Mayan children and tried to imagine what my daughter would look like. "Do Guatemalan children have fair skin? Blue eyes?" our social worker asked one day.

"No?" I answered. (Was it a trick question?)

"Actually, some do. Most of the kids will look traditionally Guatemalan, but there are many mixed-race orphans in Guatemala too. I've met children once in a long while with blue eyes. Latino kids with freckles."

I didn't care what she'd look like. I knew, just as was the case with my older three, she would be beautiful—and extraordinary—in my eyes. The agency that had completed our home study didn't yet have a direct placement program in Guatemala, so they connected us with a partner adoption agency there. On its website was a waiting child list . . . with photos.

In case you haven't heard, prospective adoptive parents are advised never to look at photo listings. For those who don't yet have a relationship with an agency, an online photo listing of children is a bad place to start. Families are advised to choose an agency because it has met their high standards of ethics, because it is well established, and because preliminary meetings or phone calls with adoption facilitators have proven that the agency is a good fit with them. They shouldn't choose an agency on the basis of a child they have seen on its website.

I knew the dangers of looking at a photo listing. Sometimes such pictures are dated. Prospective parents fall in love with a child, but the child pictured has long since been adopted by another family. Sometimes the child is much older or sicker than she appears to be in her picture. Or perhaps he is no longer able to be placed for adoption because his birthmother has changed her mind. Some disreputable or fledgling adoption agencies post pictures of children with whom they don't even have relationships in order to engage prospective adoptive parents with their agencies. It is wise, then, to start the adoption process with a well-respected agency, not with a child's picture.

But we already were signed up with this agency and had the canceled check to prove it. I skimmed through the pictures of past clients and their Guatemalan-born children and I clicked through the pages of waiting children.

Things were beginning to feel more real.

One baby girl on the agency's photo listing was older than the rest. Her picture held me captive. She had inky black hair that stood on end, as though someone had just pulled a cap off her head. Her skin glowed, her cheeks were full and rosy, and she gazed directly into the camera. Her raised left hand somehow looked like a wave. (Was she waving at me?) Her birth date was listed and she was two years younger than Isabel, just the age we'd hoped she might be. I copied the picture and set it as the wallpaper on my desktop.

"Hey," my husband said, looking over my shoulder. "You shouldn't do that. We're not supposed to do that."

I knew he was right. I removed the picture, pasted it into a Word document, and replaced it with a photograph of our three children. But I couldn't stop opening that document when my husband was out of the room. I loved looking at her—just her. All of the children on the site were beautiful, but this one looked familiar somehow. Like I knew her already. The others, as adorable as they were, looked like little strangers. (And wasn't she waving at me?)

The agency e-mailed us to say that our forms were in order. It was time to talk about our referral. I said we were very open but curious whether that one little girl, the one on the photo listing, had been placed yet. Did she have special medical needs? Why was she older than the others? At that time, many people chose to adopt Guatemalan-born children because the babies often were able to come home as infants. Couples who hadn't ever had a newborn baby didn't want to miss the experience of parenting a child from the earliest possible age. They wanted the full experience, the whole shebang.

Older children, like the one I couldn't keep my eyes off, would be at least a year old by the time they came home. But my husband had told me when we first discussed starting the adoption process that he was "over" the newborn phase. Having been through it three times before, the sleepless nights, the sour spit-up, the endless diapers, and the grim game of playing private investigator as you search for clues to solve the mysteries of why the baby is crying or refusing to sleep didn't hold a lot of magic for us.

The agency sent me a fax. The baby I inquired about had not been placed and did not have any known special needs. They had been caring for her since she was a few days old and knew her well. She was older because she had only just become available for adoption, only a day or so before our dossier hit their desks. Her birthmother was illiterate, they said, and worked long hours as a maid. Attempts to have her sign paperwork or attend appointments with social workers had failed for several months. Finally, the agency was able to make contact with the birthmother and ask her whether she still wanted to place the baby for adoption. She said yes; apparently she hadn't understood that she needed to continue being a part of the process after relinquishment.

The agency faxed us information about the baby, including medical reports written in Spanish. They promised to get the documents translated for us soon. Unable to wait, I faxed the reports to an acquaintance who speaks Spanish fluently. She translated them for me over the phone. The baby was healthy and alert and, like the three children to whom I'd given birth, weighed just over seven pounds when she was born. We accepted the agency's referral and showed our excited children the baby who would be their new sister.

I put her picture back up on my computer desktop and the wait began.

Waiting, people warned, would be the hard part.

8

The Waiting Is the Hardest Part

August 2002

Dear friends,

    We are excited to let you know that we've identified a little girl whom we hope to adopt. It will be months still before she's home. She is being called Maria but we will likely change her name. She lives in Guatemala in foster care. She is growing really well and at her mid-July check-up, she weighed 17 pounds. This puts her above average even on US growth charts. Her foster mother describes her as happy and the medical reports say she is in excellent "mental and physical health."

    Until she is legally adopted (and our case will be opened in Guatemalan court, we hope, in early September), her birthmother has the option at several different points to stop the adoption process. This is something for us to keep in mind.

    Please keep her in your prayers.

I pray for her health and safety and that her foster mother
will attend to her needs and delight in her.

We now knew who would be our little daughter. We planned
to name her Charlotte, a name I've always loved. Charlotte
invokes Charlotte Brontë, author of *Jane Eyre*, one of my favorite
novels. It is Charlotte A. Cavatica, the spider who not only saves
Wilbur's life in *Charlotte's Web* but who also educates him about
friendship. Bringing Charlotte home would take time. We had to
wait for the Guatemalan courts, US Immigration, and DNA testing to catch up with our hearts.

The kids, especially now that they had seen her, wanted their
sister home. At two years old, Isabel told people about her new
baby sister, carefully speaking the word, "Guatemala." Strangers
smiled at my curly-headed girl, thinking this an odd and
complicated game of pretend for such a little child. "Her name is
Charlotte," she said.

Charlotte and Isabel. The names sounded lovely together.

Ian lost his temper, saying he would go and get her and bring
her home himself. "What judges? What courts?" He demanded to
know who was holding things up.

I memorized the one photograph I had of her. ("Hi!" she
waved.) What would Charlotte be like? What would she make
of the dog? The cold weather? What size clothes she might wear?
What would make her laugh? Which of her siblings would she
attach to the soonest? Would she arrive in time for her first birthday? Looking out my front window as Theo carefully crossed the
street to play with the neighbors, my mind was elsewhere. Would
Charlotte like the swing set? What would she be like when she
was in first grade, like Theo was now?

Those days after we accepted the referral are a blur. In September, Ian went half days to preschool and Isabel stayed home with me. I busied myself with the ordinary tasks that at-home parents of young children accomplish every day. Changing diapers. Doing laundry. Playing Candy Land. Making meals. Cleaning the kitchen. Patching up scraped knees and hurt feelings. Potty-training. All the while, I knew that in a country far away, someone was spending the day caring for the baby who would be my daughter. As I checked that Ian washed his hands before he ate a snack, there was a stranger somewhere introducing new foods to Charlotte. As I carefully clipped Isabel's fingernails, there was a stranger somewhere washing my baby's face, changing her diaper, and laying her down to sleep.

I began to pray almost obsessive prayers. *Oh God. Please take care of her until I can. Don't let the people caring for her injure or abuse her. Please help them to be loving and patient. Please, please take care of her until I can do it myself.*

As weeks turned into months of waiting, I became more and more accustomed to the dull ache of having a piece of my heart very far away.

September 2002 (e-mail to adoption agency)

First, here's an update on where we are in our process: I've sent all the forms required to begin the DNA testing. We received our INS favorable statement and I also faxed your office the G-28. Can you confirm that the DNA test process has begun? Our power of attorney document is currently being authenticated at the Guatemalan Consulate in Chicago.

I'm sure you understand that our hearts are all pulling toward Maria. Like all your clients, we are incredibly eager to have her home. I know that the waiting game in this part of the adoption is treacherous. I just want to make sure that we're not prolonging it.

Please let me know anything more about what lies ahead for us in the coming months and what life is and has been like for little Maria.

Is there any chance at this point she could be home by Christmas?

Best from,

Jennifer

The process seemed to be slowing. If all this was God's plan, why did we still not have our next set of approvals?

I tried to keep a good attitude, and I started every day with hope. I'd pour a cup of coffee into my new favorite mug. It was oversized, red and white–painted Italian pottery. I would warm my hands around it, take a slow sip, and muster my optimism. "Today it will come," I'd say to myself. "The phone will ring. They'll tell me that she is my daughter—legally, officially, and without conditions. I'll fly to Guatemala in a day or two to bring home my baby."

I'd take a deep breath and begin the day's routine. I'd get the kids dressed and fed. I'd pack up backpacks and drop off Theo at school for first grade. I'd take Ian to preschool and spend the morning with Isabel. We'd go to the library, the post office, the grocery store. At home again, I'd check our phone messages and hurry to my desk to check e-mail before unloading the bags, ever hungry for snippets of news from the agency about my faraway baby.

I tried to excise my nervous energy with cleanser and soap bubbles and sponges. I cleaned out the refrigerator. Isabel squirted our walls and windows with water and wiped them with paper towels while I washed baseboards. Months passed. We folded laundry, raked leaves, sang the alphabet song, salted the sidewalk to melt the ice, filled the birdfeeder, put away the Christmas decorations.

Usually by midday, my cheerful, productive mood began to feel forced. Theo came home every day for lunch, and I made the kids lunches I could prepare in my sleep—macaroni and cheese, peanut butter and jelly sandwiches, yogurt and granola. They asked when their sister was coming home from Guatemala, acknowledging the gray cloud that surrounded me like a shroud as the months of waiting continued. I vacillated in my answers.

"Soon," I'd say sometimes, hoping it was true.

"Sometime," I would murmur at other times.

"I don't know," I'd whisper once in a while.

The sun lowered itself behind the neighbors' houses; evening came. David returned home from work. We ate dinner, bathed the children, read them books, and then tucked them in for the night. David and I talked about our days, filled the washer with dirty clothes, and put away books and shoes and toys.

By bedtime, disappointment had settled on my heart like a boulder. I longed to begin the work of weaving us together. I wanted to be done with the suspense and the middle-of-the-night questioning that cost me my sleep. It was silent and obsessive: *How will she adjust? Will the other children be okay? Will she be healthy? Will she be able to accept the love we have for her or will she be locked in grief over all she's lost? Will her racial difference matter? (To her? To us? To those around us?) Will I know how to parent four children? Is everything going to be all right?*

My chest strained under the weight of missing a daughter I hadn't yet met.

• • •

Agencies warn you: the adoption process is unpredictable. Regardless of how diligent they are, agencies are not in control. Schedules can slip. Documentation can get lost. Birthmothers can change their minds. Foreign governments can close their programs, change their fees, or halt all adoptions for indeterminate periods. A few months into our wait, a teachers' strike in Guatemala City closed offices and roads and prevented some of our documents from getting where they needed to be on a certain day. The Christmas holidays pushed us back several weeks. A document with a smudged signature had to be replaced. A judge who was handling our case moved to a new job. The process was out of our control.

Life went on—seasons changed, Theo began losing his baby teeth, and Isabel moved from a crib into a bed. I had days when I was at peace, certain that our baby would come home when she was meant to be with us. But more often, I struggled with the wait.

If I couldn't sit through an hour in the sun as a teenager, hoping for a tan, imagine my restlessness waiting for a child I longed to hold. I worried over her well-being. On waiting parent message boards, I read distraught waiting parents' reports of finding that their child had been abused or was receiving poor care. The stories haunted me.

Please, please God. Take care of her until I can do it myself. Please.

Having a child—whether by birth or adoption—is a risk. No parent is guaranteed an easy time bringing a child into the family. No one is guaranteed a child who is healthy or gifted or easy to parent. There are moments when accepting that lack of control makes being a parent easier—and times when it doesn't. But for some adoptive parents, Tom Petty's line about the waiting being "the hardest part" might be true.

● ● ●

I like happy endings, reconciliations, and stories of redemption. That probably explains, in large part, my love of old musicals. *On the Town. High Society. Take Me Out to the Ballgame.* Regardless of the shenanigans Gene Kelly or Frank Sinatra get into, it all works out in the end. Accepting that life, by default, is much more painful and complicated than those screenplays has been a long process for me, but adopting my daughter gave me an education that finally convinced me. Friends had attempted to persuade me of the same for decades. Like my friend Andrea, for instance.

I met Andrea when I was fifteen. We both had summer jobs at a camp in the north woods of Wisconsin. That summer I experienced my first taste of that heady, adolescent realization that I had the power to recreate myself in new environments. I could magnify my best qualities and stuff anything banal or uninviting back into my duffle bag to be disposed of before I took the bus back home.

I had recently seen the movie *Gandhi* and decided that his life and work made more sense than most of what I saw around me in the affluent suburb where I lived. I wanted to imitate his simplicity. For camp, I packed jeans, a few plain T-shirts, rain boots, flip-flops, and what I called my "Gandhi shoes." The Gandhi shoes were inexpensive, beige canvas shoes with rubber soles. (You know, like something Gandhi would have worn. That is, if somehow Gandhi had scoured the shoe aisles at Kmart for the humblest, most practical and Gandhi-esque shoes available.)

I brought little else, other than books. Yes, they were books I wanted to read, but perhaps more importantly, they were ones that helped to define who I wanted to be that summer: *The Genesee Diary* by Henri Nouwen, John Donne's poems, and a few Fitzgerald and Hemingway novels. All the books were favorites of mine, but I'd carefully selected them as props of a sort. They all would support the version of me that I was promoting that summer. (I hadn't brought any back issues of *People* magazine, for instance.)

Every day at camp, after my responsibilities as "Jenni Craftshop" were met for the day, I sat in the sun in front of my dorm reading. I first met Andrea when she walked past my reading spot. The first thing I saw was her shoes—they were Gandhi shoes, identical to mine. At the same moment I noticed her shoes, she noticed the book I held.

"Donne? I love Donne." She sat down.

"I like your shoes."

She looked at the ones I was wearing and laughed.

"What poem is it?"

I read her the lines on the page that was open in my lap:

> Batter my heart, three-person'd God, for you
> As yet but knock, breathe, shine, and seek to mend;
> That I may rise and stand, o'erthrow me, and bend
> Your force to break, blow, burn, and make me new.[1]

Thus began our friendship. Andrea is the same Andrea who saw that first picture of Isabel screaming her head off in the moment after she was born, and said: "Uh-oh. *This* is going to be interesting." I learned that we had a lot in common. She lived in the town next to mine. We both had older brothers and loved the music of Bruce Cockburn. We clicked. I liked that she was three years older, was admired at camp, and was at home in the woods. She could name every tree just by glancing at its leaves or the way its bark stretched around the trunk. She was tanned, lean, and strong. And her boyfriend? Well, getting to know Jim in all his six-foot-something tallness and with his easy swagger made me long to be older and to be able to have cool, handsome men like this in my life. The three of us feasted on strawberries, sour cream, and brown sugar that summer. We snuck out and went on night hikes with other friends and sometimes even stripped down to our underwear and swam across the lake to one of the cabins for illegal, late-night chats about God, friendship, and the meaning of life. We huddled in blankets, talking and drinking hot chocolate before swimming back again. It was a magical summer.

When we returned home that fall, I met Andrea's mother, Mildred. Mildred was a mighty woman, despite the fact that she probably never topped a hundred pounds. She seemed to me like a time traveler from pioneer days. She could quilt, she could "put up" vegetables, and she never minced words. She did, however, spell some of them out.

"That girl is not very p-r-e-t-t-y," she'd say. Or, "He is a kind person," she might say. "But not extremely s-m-a-r-t." Mildred was not unkind, just stating the facts. Spelling out such observations softened them somehow.

It was Mildred, by the way, who more than twenty years after

I met her, patiently taught me to sew my first—and let's be honest, *only*—quilt when I was pregnant with Theo. This was the one that I'd thought would be my baby's "lovey" but has ended up being a plaything for my girls, a picnic blanket for their American Girl dolls.

I cherished the quilt-making afternoons when Mildred, Andrea, and I drank tea, pieced together the quilt, and talked about the nature of life and about which babies were, and which babies were not, c-u-t-e.

I'm still pleased to remember that Mildred approved of my wedding—and not just because her daughter was my maid of honor. Years later Andrea told me that her mother judged subsequent weddings against mine: "It was fine, but it wasn't a 'Jennifer Grant' wedding." She also teased me, calling me "Typhoid Mary" after I stood up for Andrea in her wedding while sick with the flu. Later, Andrea and her husband, Michael, would suffer through their form of the virus on their honeymoon.

"You might want to give Typhoid Mary a call," Andrea would quote her mother to me, years later. "I hear she's in town."

From Mildred, Andrea inherited her strength and wry sense of humor. She is a woman of faith and continues to echo her mother's stoic acceptance that "life is hard."

This was the one point about which Andrea and I would argue, right from the start of our friendship.

"Life is *good*," I often said. (I should have started my own clothing line.)

"Life is *hard*," Andrea would answer. "That is just the way it is."

When she uttered such pronouncements, my attention was yanked away from Bryan Adams singing "Straight from the Heart" on the radio or from the deep blue of her boyfriend Jim's eyes. I felt like her perspective was impossibly antique. I pictured her standing on some windy plain, the hem of her calico dress flapping around her shins after she'd just lost a year's worth of harvest when the barn burned down.

I didn't want to accept that life was hard. After all, I wasn't a coal miner, for crying out loud. I was determined to make my adulthood happy. I'd weathered my parents' divorce and the way my troubled—and much-loved—sister would come in and out of our family's life while I was growing up. (Who could make me laugh the way my sister Sue could? No one.) These things were out of my control, but I knew that as I moved toward adulthood, I could start constructing my own life. I pictured my childhood disappearing back into the distance behind me with every passing year.

I knew that life wouldn't be a party every day, but I was determined that it would be tangle-free, calm, and filled with ordinary joys. My faith would continue to grow. My relationships would be healthy. I'd maintain an appropriate balance between the material things I wanted and the scarcities I knew existed in the world. Like Gandhi, I'd travel light and live true. Tragedy, extended heartache and the aftershocks of bad decisions wouldn't haunt me. Despite memorizing Donne's powerful sonnet, I didn't really want God to batter my heart at all. I felt like it already had been assaulted when I was a child. Instead I wanted God to heal it, strengthen it, and honor the hope that lived in it.

It took me a very long time to shake off the idea that if I watched closely and chose the details of my life carefully, I could avoid the potholes and broken glass on the proverbial sidewalk that seemed to trip up so many people around me. I learned that there is no avoiding suffering and disappointment, no matter how carefully we plan our lives, no matter what good decisions we make, regardless of whether we are trying to follow after God. The very last vestige of my adolescent hope that I could sidestep suffering was the painful wait for my daughter to come home.

9

Meeting Mia

In November, our agency sent us an e-mail to alert us that our daughter's case would require at least a few more months before it went to the attorney general's office, the *Procuradoria General de la Nacion*, known as PGN. In Guatemalan adoptions, PGN is the final stop. The Christmas holidays close down the Guatemalan courts for several weeks, the e-mail explained, so we were now "looking at" a longer wait. Our daughter would be older on her homecoming than we had expected.

I thought about all the attention and care I had given to my other children during their infancies. Would my daughter, as an older child, ever bond with me? Would she have learned patterns of behavior that I would have to disrupt? What if her attachment with her foster mother was so strong that coming home to us would irreparably break her heart?

I also began to question our choice to name her Charlotte. Her foster family called her Maria, the name we believe her birth-mother gave her and a name commonly used in Latin America to honor the Virgin Mary. Would it be fair to bring a child home to a new land and immediately change her name so radically?

We thought of keeping Maria as her name, but it didn't feel right. We had close friends whose daughter was Maria and when I thought of the name, their dear little two-year-old's face popped into my mind. I saw her pretty almond eyes and heard her low, raspy voice. "Hey, Brenda Vaccaro," we used to say when little Maria asked for a sippy cup or cracker.

One day it came to me. We should call our new daughter "Mia," a name I had always loved. Mia, after all, is a form of Maria and would be a way to acknowledge the name her birthmother had given her. In Italian and Spanish, it means "mine." My little girl. My Mia.

Mia would not be home by Thanksgiving, Christmas, or maybe even her first birthday in February. I felt almost desperate to see her. The agency e-mailed us brief updates and pictures every few months, but I needed to see her with my own eyes. I needed to get a sense of who she was and learn more about what her care was like.

My friend Laurie, late of the church book club, works for an airline and offered to add David and me to her guest travelers list, allowing us to buy discounted tickets to Guatemala City. Because a DNA test had established maternity and because her birthmother had signed off on the adoption for the fourth and final time, we were permitted to visit Mia. We couldn't leave the country with her—and indeed were advised not to leave the hotel—but we were told we could keep her overnight and spend a few days with her. The thought floored me, lifted my spirits, and I was overflowing with gratitude for my generous friend Laurie. Could it be that I'd soon be able to meet Mia, the girl I already loved?

About a week later, David and I found ourselves in a luxury hotel in Guatemala City. Palm trees lined the circular drive. The lobby floor was inlaid marble, brown and gold. On the carved wood reception desk and tables around the room were vases filled with huge bouquets of flowers. The flowers were other-worldly: the orange birds of paradise looked like the work of a gifted origami artist. Speckled orchids perched atop thin stems. The red, heart-shaped leaves of anthuriums bowed down over the sides of their vases. Despite the opulent room, I kept my gaze on the large clock above the reception desk. It was reminiscent of a grand train station in another time and place. Its Roman numerals and black hands kept me mesmerized. We were min-utes away from meeting Mia.

David and I sat down on a sofa, then stood, then sat again. People entered the lobby from elevators or the adjacent restau-rants and then exited through the front doors across the room from us. Others entered the hotel from the street. It was these people, backlit by the bright morning sun, whom we scrutinized. Those who pushed a stroller or held a baby made our hearts quicken as we waited to meet a baby who both was, and was not, our daughter.

We had arrived the night before, leaving the kids with David's parents. It was dark when we arrived, and the quick taxi ride from the airport left me with few impressions of the city. We went straight to our room, ordered a meal, and waited the last long night to meet our baby.

Finally, about a half hour later than expected, I saw Mia as her foster mother carried her into the lobby. She was nine months old and wore a lime green dress with a green ribbon sash and a matching hat. Her big black eyes were wide and unblinking.

Much later, I would understand that glazed look was her response to unfamiliar people and environments.

We sat with the foster mother, a woman also named Maria, in the lobby. I didn't want to overwhelm Mia, so as much as I wanted to grab her and whisk her upstairs to our room, I thought spending a few minutes together might make the transition from her foster mother to my arms easier. I showed Maria pictures of Theo, Ian, and Isabel, now ages two, four, and six. I thought it might be a comfort to her to know we were parents already and could keep this baby safe and healthy for the next two days.

Through a translator employed by the hotel, Maria told us that she had cared for many babies as a foster mother, but that Mia was "the sweetest of the sweet." After about twenty minutes, she unpacked a bag that contained two baby bottles, a package of powdered milk, and a bag of white sugar. She set it all on a table in the lobby and, with the help of the translator, taught us how to make Mia's formula. She said to spoon seven or eight heaping tablespoons of white sugar into the bottle, add a scoop of powdered milk, and then fill with purified water and shake.

I tried to act casual. My daughter consumed that much sugar . . . multiple times a day? What could this be doing to her teeth?

To think of how I had fed my older kids when they were younger. The brown rice cereal mixed with breast milk. Organic sweet potatoes. Sippy cups filled with juice so diluted that it could be mistaken for water.

Toto, I've a feeling we're not in Kansas anymore, I thought.

Theo was older than two when he had his first refined sugar. To him, "dessert" was a small wedge of brie and several slices of a pear.

"Dessert, Mommy?" he'd ask, and I would prepare a little plate for him.

He was three or so when, in what is now a famous story in our family lore, we were at Mark and Mary's house and a package of Oreos was sitting open on the counter.

"Jen, can he have one?" Mary asked, knowing what "dessert" had meant to Theo thus far in his life and likely pitying the poor boy.

"Sure, why not?"

Mark, Mary, and I watched closely as Theo lifted the cookie to his mouth. He took a tiny bite and, a moment later, let out a great sigh of pleasure.

"Are these always available?" he asked.

We still say it to each other, when something is particularly delicious.

Are these always available?

But sitting in the lobby of this fancy hotel in Guatemala City, I learned that Mia was getting refined sugar by the cupful and she was only nine months old. I understood that a chubby baby signaled a healthy baby in a country where malnourishment and disease took so many children's lives. There were more important concerns here than raising kids with sophisticated palettes or making sure they had perfect checkups at the dentist. Mia's foster mother fed her and kept her healthy. I knew I should be grateful for that, as well as for the trusting, peaceful relationship they had.

I took a deep breath and put the bottles back into the bag to take upstairs.

After Maria reluctantly released Mia into our arms, we went up to our room. I was thrilled to be alone with her and bemused by the calm way she regarded us. The fancy green dress had to go—I wanted to change her clothes into an outfit I'd chosen. Under the lime green dress, I discovered layer after layer of clothing. Finally she was just wearing a onesie, sitting up straight on the bedspread. I wanted to look her over, the way a mother counts the fingers and toes of her newborn baby. Her skin was a beautiful caramel color and deliciously soft. She smelled clean, like baby soap. I breathed her in.

At the top of her left arm, I found two small, straight scars about the width of a staple and close together. *What had happened to her?* I wondered. They looked like they had been deliberately made. Was it a tradition among the indigenous people to mark a baby this way? Later I would learn that these scars were the result of a Bacillus Calmette-Guerin, or BCG, vaccination to protect against tuberculosis. I still don't know why there are two—perhaps the person who gave her the vaccination feared that it hadn't taken the first time.

Bluish-black spots on her back also startled me. Were they bruises? Was Maria less gentle than she seemed? I then remembered reading that birthmarks on babies with darker complexions often look like bruises. Would people see these after Mia's homecoming and think she had been abused?

After examining her little body, I got her dressed and began the happy labor of simply enjoying her. Over the course of the next forty-eight hours, I shed the anxiety about her well-being that had plagued me for months. I felt confident that she and I would bond easily when she came home, whenever that was. David and I talked to her, played, and took pictures and videos to show our children at home.

The first afternoon, she made it clear that only I was allowed to hold her. It wasn't that she didn't like David. In fact, she whined when he left the room. But she granted me the right to hold her. For meals, we brought her down to the restaurant in the hotel lobby and fed her bits of rice and minced fruits and vegetables. We played peekaboo with large linen napkins and were delighted to make her laugh. When we laid her in a crib, she quickly dropped off to sleep. But, although I had reluctantly made the sugary formula for her, she would not take a bottle from either David or me.

Two days later, we again met Maria in the hotel lobby. Maria looked relieved to see Mia, and the baby quickly went to her, obviously happy to be once again with the only mother she knew. David and I packed our bags. We dropped off a large suitcase full of baby vitamins, clothing, and diapers to our agency for the orphanage it supported. We bought souvenirs at a shop in the basement of the hotel and took a taxi back to the airport.

It was surreal to meet Mia so briefly and then leave her behind, so far from home.

I wrote an e-mail to update our family and friends about our trip.

November 2002

Hey everybody,

We are home today from our long weekend in Guatemala City. It was in the low seventies when we flew out this morning and is snowing here tonight.

We had a wonderful visit with Mia. She is now nine months old. We were able to spend Friday and Saturday with her and she slept over in our hotel room Friday night. She is a happy, secure baby who is doted on by her foster mother. She's been in her foster mother's home since she was only a few days old and they are clearly bonded with each other.

We were happy to see that Mia seems to be on track developmentally. She babbles, sits well, imitates behavior, and has a lot of fun. She seemed content with us, but seemed to miss her foster mother at night. She never let us feed her the bottle, just turned her face away when we tried. Maybe that is a special time of day she associates only with her foster mother—and who were we, anyway? So we let her drink from a cup (which she seemed to know how to do) and fed her with a spoon.

I felt full of gratitude when I was with her. I felt strongly that my (and, collectively, all of our) prayers have been answered. She is happy and well fed and is a wonderful little girl.

We so look forward to her coming home, whenever that will be. For those of you who know the lingo, we're still in family court, stalled as we wait for a social worker there to review our documents.

Knowing how well she is doing has eased my worries.

Love,

Jen

Thanksgiving came and went. Then Christmas. Then the new year. There were rumors on message boards and websites that Guatemala might discontinue its program because of continued reports of unethical adoptions. Some families who had started the adoption process after we did already had brought their babies home. This, of course, concerned me.

Dear God, remember when I used to recite that Donne poem when I was in high school and college? Asking you to "batter" my heart? I take it all back. Please just let my Mia come home. Amen.

On message boards, waiting parents were increasingly

posting about their fears that the courts would suspend adoptions and that their children would be left in limbo there. Some of the babies seemed to be moving unexpectedly from foster home to foster home. What was going on? Would Mia's adoption come through, or would we find ourselves in some nightmarish scenario where everything but the final approval from PGN had been granted?

It seemed ironic and unjust that as rumors of fraudulent or "rubber-stamped" adoptions (greased by the almighty dollar, or, more appropriately, the almighty *quetzal*) increased and threatened to close the courts, everyone working on our case seemed excessively particular.

The sense of peace that I'd found on our visit in November had worn thin by March.

I started praying my obsessive prayers again: *Please God. Please bring her home before anything changes with adoptions in Guatemala. Please keep her safe and healthy until I can take care of her. Please take care of her until I can take care of her myself.*

Why did this have to be so hard?

February 2003

Dear All,

You are all so kind to us. Thank you for prayers for Mia's well-being and for us to have patience. We are truly rich in our friends. Mia's first birthday is Friday and approaching that day and knowing she won't be home for it has been hard on me. It stings to miss another significant date in her life.

We'll just have to have a big celebration for her baptism!

But here's some good news. Today we learned that we are

(finally) out of family court. My contact at our agency said she expects we'll enter final court (also known as "PGN") this week.

PGN is the trickiest stage. Some people fly through in three days, other cases take months. It seems that depending on a lot of factors (including corruption and the court's workload), cases are tossed out or green-lighted. If a case is rejected for something minor such as a typo, the case must start at the beginning of the final court process again. Sometimes cases are rejected due to questionable documentation or suspicions over the legitimacy of the adoption. I have paged through our dossier and all the documents we have submitted and everything seems to be in very good order. All to say, please keep us in your prayers as we enter the dreaded PGN.

Our most recent medical update was great. Mia is very tall and healthy. Her height is atypical for Guatemalan children and will put her in good stead with her big sister, Isabel. That she is tall feels like another sign that she is just the right girl for our family.

Love,

Jen

In the next set of pictures, the first we'd received since Christmas, I noticed that Mia didn't look well. Her face looked pale and she had what appeared to be sores on her face. Her eyes looked swollen, as though she had been crying. I e-mailed the agency to ask if she was still in Maria's care and whether she was healthy. My e-mail went unread for a few days due to power outages in Guatemala City.

Please, please, God, take care of her until I can take care of her myself, I prayed for the hundredth time. But then, in a still moment, a thought settled itself in my mind.

I am taking care of her.

She is My child even more than she is yours.

And even when she is home with you, I will still be the one who is caring for her.

I understood.

And then I remembered about a dozen times over the last months when I believe God was trying to send me a comforting message, but I was too busy voicing my anxiety and fears to hear it. A time when I was lost in worry at an amusement park with my kids and the music playing from the merry-go-round was "Maria" from *West Side Story.* I had stopped worrying for a moment and listened to the song, smiling and remembering that when I first saw her picture on the photo listing, I had hummed that song to myself.

Or, months later, when I was nearly in tears in the produce section of the grocery store, wondering whether Guatemalan courts would suspend adoptions, I focused on the music playing over the store's intercom. It was "Danny's Song" by Kenny Loggins, a favorite of mine when I was a girl and a song that for some odd reason always filled me with hope.

For the rest of the day those lyrics stayed with me, that promise that everything was going to be all right. (You know you're getting old when you love the Muzak at the grocery store.)

Or the happy accident of chatting with another mother at the park one day and realizing, when her son came running over to her, that he was Guatemalan-born. "I'm waiting for my daughter. She's in Guatemala," I sputtered.

"Oh, we adopted our son from there too," she said.

The little boy grinned at me and I said, "Guatemala's great."

He nodded and skipped off to the swings.

I'm not usually the type of person who thanks God for optimal parking spots or good hair days, but I believe there were times I missed God's hints that everything was going to be all right. (Oh, and the reason Mia had been pale and had sores on her face was that she was just getting over chicken pox. When the electricity came back on in Guatemala City, the agency e-mailed me to let me know.)

Chicken pox. Okay, that's benign enough.

Waiting for our adoption to come through was a long, dark passage for me. Going through it, I learned how hard it was for me to release my fears and give them to God.

I also had to admit that, at times, life could be very, very hard.

10

Homecoming

April 2003

Hey everyone,

Today our adoption of Mia was approved in PGN, the attorney general's office in Guatemala City! Mia is officially our daughter. We will travel in a few weeks to bring her home. Before we go, documents in Guatemala must be translated, she will be issued a new birth certificate and US passport and so on. I pray that those steps go smoothly.

The kids cheered and jumped for joy and fell over in a big three-way hug when we got the good news at lunchtime.

Much love (and joy and relief),

Jen

We finally got "the call" in April 2003 and traveled to Guatemala City a few days before Mother's Day. It had been six months since our visit to meet Mia. I wondered whether she would remember us and how much she had changed.

David and I arrived at night, went almost directly to bed, and met our translator in the hotel lobby before six the following morning. We were driven to the US embassy, where Maria, Mia's foster mother, was already standing out in the chilly morning, waiting for us. Mia looked sleepy but comfortable, snuggled in Maria's arms. She and Maria, her foster mother told me, had to get up very early that day to catch a bus from Antigua. I wish I had known and could have sent money for a taxi.

Mia was much taller now and no longer the baby we met in November, but a toddler. Her arm was wrapped around the back of her foster mother's neck, and throughout the morning, she stroked Maria's hair and affectionately twisted it around her fingers. (Would she ever do that to my hair?) She regarded us with the blank look I still sometimes see when she meets a stranger or is in an unfamiliar place. She was wrapped in the pink, printed blanket, the one that I'd seen over the months in pictures and that she had slept with when she stayed at our hotel in November. Later that morning, I would beg her foster mother to leave it with us.

The translator pulled us into a tiny store where Mia's new passport pictures were taken in the space of about twenty seconds. She was jostled, handed from the foster mother to the translator to the photographer. She began to cry but soon was calm again.

The embassy wasn't open yet, but our translator said if we arrived early, we would be more likely to get a morning appointment and "get out of there." Once the embassy opened, she hurried us inside and gestured for us to sit in molded plastic chairs. Mia stayed in her foster mother's lap and I tried to connect with her, handing her toys and a bottle. She regarded me neutrally—unaware of how my heart was racing in my chest. A little while later, we were called to appear before the embassy official, and David, Mia, and I entered a room that felt no bigger than a walk-in closet.

By 8:30 a.m., all the paperwork was complete. She was officially our child, and the agent in that tiny, final room said that our country promised to embrace her as a US citizen on her arrival in America. I could have waved a flag or sung the national anthem, I felt so patriotic. I was aware that the opportunities for health, education, and a future had just opened to this tiny girl in ways so many people around the globe only dream about.

We invited Maria to join us for breakfast at our hotel. At the restaurant, Mia sat in my lap, a white cloth napkin tied around her neck as a makeshift bib. I was fascinated by her every move. She ate the mango, pineapple, and watermelon that I'd cut into small pieces for her. When she was finished, she began stirring the fruit together on my plate, mixing it with the black beans. We all laughed at the mess she made. Sometimes I was able to ask an English-speaking waiter to translate a sentence or two for us. But mostly we all sat in silence, smiling at the baby.

"Has she been well?" we asked Maria through our waiter-translator.

"Yes. Very healthy," was the waiter's translation before he rushed away from our table again. It was a message at odds with the bagful of prescription medicines Maria instructed us to give her.

"Is she talking?" I asked later.

"Yes, a little. She says words like *Mama*." Mama. My heart clenched inside me, aware again of the loss Mia was about to sustain. I wondered whether she would ever think of me as her mama.

After breakfast, we sat in the hotel lobby for a few minutes and said good-bye to Maria. It was there that I retrieved another translator from the hotel's business center to make sure we could communicate a few final thoughts. First I asked for the pink baby blanket. We then thanked Maria for her loving care of Mia and gave her an envelope containing a few hundred dollars. Later Maria would tell us, via e-mail, that she used the money to help pay for her daughter's wedding.

Before she left, Maria began to cry. Hard. With the help of the translator, she explained that she had taken care of many babies, but never for so long a period of time. It was hard for her to let Mia go.

Finally, we had a last hug, Maria gave Mia one last kiss, and we said good-bye.

Our new daughter went with us easily; the novelty of the hotel and its indoor fountain, shiny elevator, and oversized vases full of flowers likely distracted her.

The rest of the day passed in a blur. We brought Mia upstairs and changed her clothes. We watched her while she napped. When we laid her down in the crib, she smiled at us politely as though she was treating inexperienced babysitters with courtesy. We ventured out of the hotel to nearby shops, aware of the guards armed with machine guns standing around high-end shops and in hotel lobbies. I knew anger, corruption, and violence were lurking in the city, just out of our sight. I was eager to get our daughter home.

The next day, the three of us were calm and quiet travelers.

As we cleared security and moved into the concourse at La Aurora International Airport, it was excruciating to think of all that Mia was leaving behind. A birth family she did not know. Physical connection to the Mayan people and their ancient, luminous culture. A language she had only begun to speak. The comfort of Maria and the only home she had ever known.

But she was leaving other things too. Her orphan status. Prejudice that would exclude her from education. The sickness, malnutrition, natural disasters, violence, and poverty that plague the nation.

Meanwhile, Mia looked around at the bright lights, the upscale jewelry stores and Duty-Free shops, and the passing faces of people hurrying by on other journeys. She looked interested and even happy.

Our port of entry into the United States was Houston. The moment we landed, Mia officially became a citizen of the United States. Sitting in the waiting area near the immigration lines at the airport, I looked around at all the newly formed families of American parents and Guatemalan-born children. Here we were, just beginning our lives together. There were doubts, there was anxiety, there was an awareness of the great loss the children had suffered, but there was great happiness, too, in the knowledge that this first part of our journeys as families had successfully come to an end.

May 2003

We're home!

It's getting late, but I wanted to let you know that we've made our quick trip to Guatemala and Mia is home! We flew in Wednesday night and flew out on Friday morning. Thursday was so fast and full a day. It started with our appointment at the embassy, breakfast with Mia's foster mother, and then a more relaxed time in and around our hotel.

I've been reading a lot about toddler adoption and I think that the shared time we had with her foster mother helped Mia to feel a bit more comfortable with us. When we said good-bye the foster mother really cried but Mia didn't understand and happily went with us. She is serene and happy and obviously well-loved.

She is walking a little bit, but mostly loves to be held. We took turns wearing her in the sling. She went to bed about 9 p.m. and slept until we had to get her up to go to the airport at about 5:45 a.m. She woke up smiling.

I was moved by the fact that she had no idea that she was leaving all she has known when we got on the plane. Everything's changed for her. She's an American citizen. She has a big family. My heart goes out to her about leaving everything familiar behind.

Tonight Theo kept saying, "She's so brave."

She was happy with us at home tonight, unless I left the room or turned my back. At those points, she began to cry. But mostly, she was talking and laughing and completely in love with the other kids. Theo is smitten with her and fed her two yogurts. She would take a bite and then say "mas" to ask for more. Ian sang a number of impromptu songs about how much he loves babies and loves being a big brother. Isabel is a little unsure in the way that youngest kids are when a new sibling gets home . . . she alternates between being very sweet to her (offered her special blanket and doll to Mia when she cried) and acting a little aloof. I gave the two of them a tub tonight and she was dear with Mia. We are all still getting to know each other, but tonight was a good introduction to new family for all of us.

Thanks for all your kindness to us through this process.

Love,

Jen (Mia's Mom!)

Part Three
Learning to Know

11

Honeymooners

My husband's grandmother Rhoda is from central Pennsylvania. Her parents—and those of her husband—were members of the Brethren in Christ church. As "Plain People," they were not Amish exactly, but there were similarities. The women wore head coverings. Buttons on clothing were hidden. They lived pious and frugal lives. In Rhoda's generation, however, things loosened up a bit. People started showing their shirt buttons. The women started wearing lipstick and dresses that showed off their shapely selves. (And let me tell you, when her future husband, Stanley, first saw Rhoda at a tent meeting, she sure was shapely. He would blush to remember it his whole life long.) Also in Rhoda's generation—yank!—women's head coverings came off. As much as she has changed from her parents' way of life, however, Rhoda's roots show. Her faith is grounded and sure. She's somehow both frugal and openhanded in her generosity.

I love the remnants of her Pennsylvania Dutch culture. At ninety, she still makes us jars of pickled vegetables—red beets and vegetable *chow chow*. She doesn't say that a baby is whining, but is "grexing." And when she meets new people, she'll often say she's pleased to "learn to know them." Learning to know. Those extra words make all the difference. That is, an hour after being introduced to total strangers, how can we say, "Glad to know you"? How can you know *anyone* after so little time? After more than two decades of marriage, I would hesitate to say I fully know my husband; I'm still *learning* to know him.

The summer we brought Mia home was a heightened time of "learning to know" her. Here was a fully developed little person who, somehow, was as much a part of the family as any of the rest of us. Grexing and all.

A few days after we arrived home from Guatemala City, I took Mia with me to a volunteer appreciation lunch at Theo's school. During his first grade year, while waiting to hear that Mia's adoption had been finalized, I served as "art appreciation mom" for his class. I also came into the classroom to read with kids who were struggling. I helped at the holiday parties, showing kids how to turn each other into mummies with rolls of toilet paper at the Halloween party, tossing beanbags into "Bozo's Buckets" at Christmas, and playing conversation heart Bingo at Valentine's Day. Throwing myself into volunteering at his school had helped to distract me from the excruciating wait.

Also, and not insignificantly, I was a first-time elementary school mom. I was energetic, creative, and eager to be involved. Sometimes I even went to PTA meetings! In the evening! Now that I have four kids in three different schools, I'm not as involved at the elementary school. (Or any school, for that matter.) I imagine the younger moms look at me sideways when I arrive with a store-bought Greek salad for the teacher appreciation luncheon or with boxes of Dove bars for birthday treats. Who can blame them for judging jaded moms like me, especially after they were up half the night decorating homemade shortbread with the initials of each student in their child's class?

I understand; I used to be just the same way. But be forewarned, young moms: there will come a time when you, too, start bringing packaged snacks to the holiday party. You too will skip PTA meetings and volunteer luncheons. You too will be only vaguely aware of which of your daughter's friends are in her class or that she has a student teacher this month.

You don't believe me?

Well, just you wait!

But back then, I was on board. Sure my daughter had only been home for two days. Sure I was exhausted emotionally and there were mounds of laundry and a multitude of other chores to do. But I did not want to miss it. (The teachers were making salads and desserts! They decorated the library! We even would probably get a little swag, like a pin or a bookmark!) I got a sitter for Ian and Isabel, clicked Mia into her car seat, and was at the school by noon.

I had been a "sling mama" with my other kids from their earliest days, and although Mia was almost thirty pounds and already a toddler, I thought I'd wear her in the sling as well. Well, for as long as I could, anyway. I parked the car, slipped on the sling, and tucked her into it. I felt her adjust her body and snuggle closer to me. Had she only been home two days? How could I love her so much already?

In the school library, my son's first grade teacher approached me. This man was a delight. A strict and organized teacher, he was also willing to go off-topic when one of the kids asked a question. I loved the way he reveled in helping his students learn. I introduced him to Mia, who looked at him with interest. Had she ever seen a man so tall? Had she ever seen anyone with such orange hair and fair skin?

I walked up to the long tables of salads and he stood beside me, smiling and talking to Mia. "Do you want a plate for her?" he asked, meeting her gaze. His wife was pregnant for the first time and he seemed enamored with babies.

"Oh, we'll just share," I said. I used the confident, nonchalant tone of a veteran mother, all the while knowing that I had no idea what foods she liked or whether exposure to, say, the shredded cabbage or peanuts in that Asian salad would send her into anaphylactic shock. Would she grind all of the food on my paper plate into a huge, messy glob, the way she did last week at the hotel in Guatemala City?

I had no idea.

I filled my plate, holding the serving spoons and forks where she could see them and repeated the names of each food I chose. "Blueberry. See, it's a blueberry. This is a strawberry. This is spinach. Yum!" I hoped somehow that hearing these words once would be enough to teach this tiny girl their names.

"Oh," another volunteer mom said, pointing at my plate. "Your baby must really love blueberries!"

I didn't recognize the woman. She was probably some deadbeat mom of a fifth-grader who dropped off grocery-store cupcakes one time during the year just to score an invite to this luncheon. I looked at my plate and was surprised by the mountain of berries I'd served myself.

"I really don't know. I have no idea what she likes," I said. The other mom, looking a bit concerned, shuffled away.

That day, Mia ate dozens of blueberries. I chatted with friends. I'd not seen many of them for months—I'd been too busy hiding out in my house, checking e-mail, and begging God to bring my baby home. They marveled at her sweet nature and the way we looked like we belonged together.

"Seriously, she has your eyes," my friend Becky said.

As I left the school library, I saw Theo's teacher and pointed out the purple ring around Mia's mouth. "Well, I guess she likes blueberries," I said.

That week, I spent a small fortune on blueberries, delighted to have found something she liked. Mia still wouldn't take the bottle from us and I was concerned that she might become dehydrated. She didn't seem to be drinking much. I went to the grocery store and bought every type of tropical fruit juice I could find. Guava, pineapple, papaya. I filled sippy cups with them and lined them up on the table by her high chair.

"Okay Mia, let's do this thing."

The novelty of so many choices got her drinking at least a few ounces at a time.

For her first few months home, Mia didn't like me to be out of her sight. She was happy in the sling, content to be in my lap, and went down for a nap only after I sat beside the crib and talked or sang her to sleep. But after missing her so viscerally for so many months, I was glad to have her as a constant companion. Most of the time.

June 2003

Dear Andrea,

Thanks for your note. I don't have much time to write—I keep promising myself to go to bed earlier. I forgot how tiring it can be to chase a toddler, keep her from falling down the stairs, and still try to keep some order around the house. I put up gates on the stairs, but Mia is intent on getting around them. No, life doesn't feel 100% different—what a good question, by the way. It feels like it's clipping along in its usual rhythm, except with a toddler taking things apart and making us laugh and keeping me from doing the laundry.

And she is a joy.

Oh and no, I don't yet feel like I'm an "adoptive parent," per se. I know other issues will help me to connect with that aspect of all this later but it feels more somehow that I "had" a toddler. Gave birth to? Has she not always been here? Like somehow suddenly I added one to the family.

I'm still getting to know her, learning what comforts her, what makes her laugh, what she likes. One thing that makes me sad is that, unlike with the other kids, I can't always swoop in and be the magic Mommy and say or do the perfect thing to comfort her. I just don't know her well enough yet. But it's been striking how easy it has been to envelop her into our family life. We've already eaten out at a restaurant with all four kids uneventfully and basically follow our usual routine.

Having her and knowing that we have brought someone into our family who wasn't part of a family before does make the suburban promenade easier to handle. As I make the rounds to the school and the pediatrician and to baseball games, I sometimes think that at least we're sharing all this abundance, all these good gifts with someone who didn't have any of it.

Just buying her shoes was touching to me. She came home in size 3 ? shoes and walked with a terrible lurch, the few steps she took. The day after we came home, I took her to the shoe store for a fitting and bought her new shoes. Size 6! And, not surprisingly, she walks much better already. If you held up her new white shoes with the old black ones, your stomach would drop. The old shoes look like doll shoes.

She makes all the kids laugh so hard. They really appreciate her baby-ness. The silly faces and sounds and things she does. Having four kids feels like a lot sometimes. At moments, I think: Wow these are a lot of people! Can I give each one everything he or she needs? Can I be as attentive as they need me to be?

> Much love.
>
> Off to bed,
>
> Jen

Did you ever see *About Schmidt*? The movie released late in 2002, just months before Mia's homecoming. Jack Nicholson plays Warren Schmidt, a recently widowed insurance agent who, increasingly, becomes aware of the meaninglessness of his life. The movie almost feels like an exploration of the book of Ecclesiastes: "Vanity of vanities, all is vanity. What profit has a man from all his labor in which he toils under the sun? One generation passes away, and another generation comes . . ." (Ecclesiastes 1.2–4).

Warren is lonely. His wife is gone. He has retired from a job he held for most of his adult life. He learns that his best friend has betrayed him. When Warren returns to the office to offer assistance to the person who has the job from which he just retired, it's clear he's neither welcome nor needed. Leaving the building, he catches a glimpse of his files. The boxes are stacked beside a Dumpster; the artifacts from an entire career wait to be taken out with the garbage.

What profit has a man . . .

Warren sees a television commercial for a child sponsorship program and decides to sponsor a child. Warren begins to write the child, a young Tanzanian boy named Ndugu (pronounced "En-doo-goo") Umbo. Throughout the movie, Warren's rambling letters to Ndugu expose the man's inner life. Some of what this friendless, former insurance agent tells the African boy is hilarious. He remarks that although his daughter Jeanie is past her prime, she has made a mistake in choosing her fiancé, Randall. He recommends that Ndugu pledge a fraternity when he goes to college. He sends the boy a pamphlet on Buffalo Bill Cody, as though little Ndugu might be able to wrap his mind around the Old West. The letters he writes to Ndugu are absurd when you consider the context in which the boy lives. (Well, they're poignant *and* absurd, but you have to see the movie to understand what I mean.)[1]

After Mia's homecoming, David and I often narrated certain moments, Warren Schmidt–style, as though Mia were composing letters to her foster mother in Guatemala. It helped us let off a little steam, made us laugh, and reminded us of the huge adjustment she was making.

"Dear Maria," one of us would start, attempting to imitate Jack Nicholson's Warren Schmidt, his voice deadpan and steady, tinged in sarcasm. "'Mom' has just announced that we're having 'pancakes' this morning."

(We always made big air quotes when "Mom," "Dad," "sister," or "brother," or other words that were new to her were mentioned in these imaginary letters.)

"This seems to be grounds for great excitement around here. What are 'pancakes,' you might ask? Well, at first glance they look like the tortillas you used to make for me. But, having been served them once before, I can tell you they are nothing like tortillas. Truly Maria, had I known that someday I'd be eating the kind of food 'Mom' makes here, I would have been sure to express my gratitude more enthusiastically for your wonderful culinary skills.

Returning to the issue at hand, however, if the behavior of my 'brothers' and 'sister' is any indication, 'pancakes' are not only cause for great excitement, but are made to be drowned in 'maple syrup.' This morning, 'Mom' gave a long and rather dull explanation about 'maple syrup,' saying that it comes from the insides of trees. Fascinating!

Yours very truly,
The Girl They Call Mia"

A few weeks after Mia came home, David took all four kids to the park district swimming pool. He returned a few hours later looking frazzled.

"How'd it go?" I asked.

Instead of answering me directly, he voiced, Warren Schmidt–style, the letter that he imagined Mia was writing to her foster mother about the experience:

"Dear Maria,

Today 'Dad' took us to the pool. Before we left, the 'brothers' couldn't stop saying, 'This is going to be so much fun.' Understandably, my interest was piqued. I must say, however, that I've never experienced anything quite so terrifying in my life. Picture a swimming pool crammed full of very loud, very active, very white children.

Then picture 'Dad' holding me on his hip and walking into the 'shallow' end of the pool. Shallow! I could have drowned in a second! I tried to alert as many people as possible about imminent demise. 'Dad' said I would get used to it and that it was 'fun.'

Sending greetings from paradise!

Mia"

The days sped by. The three older kids started swim lessons. The boys played baseball. I watched Mia grow accustomed to the pool and to swinging high on the swings in our backyard. For the first few weeks, Mia slept in a crib in a room with David and me, but we then moved her upstairs to the room she would share with Isabel. Sometimes Isabel would climb into Mia's crib after we had put them to bed. I could hear them laughing from downstairs. Things seemed to be going well.

That summer, we packed the van and drove to South Dakota with Mark and Mary and their two daughters for a few weeks. "We'll have the best vacation ever," Mark said.

On the way to Rapid City, we used walkie-talkies to chat and plan pit stops. (David had a cell phone by then, I think. But in 2003, he was the only adult of the four of us who did.) We played silly I Spy games between our two cars and musical minivans at gas stations and rest areas. Mia was so accustomed to my full attention that I spent most of the drive turned around in my seat, maintaining eye contact with her so that she wouldn't cry.

Our weeks there were wonderful. Mia and Ruby, Mark and Mary's younger daughter, became fast friends. All of the kids ran in a little pack. Spending my days with Mary, who had adopted two of her daughters by then, helped me gain some perspective on Mia. In the weeks prior to our vacation, I'd told Mary about a stubborn streak I'd observed in Mia, but all Mary had seen until then was my daughter's sweet nature.

After being together in South Dakota, Mary agreed that Mia could be, in the most subtle ways, quite contrary. She agreed with me that it seemed that no one had ever said "no" to her before. When I reprimanded her, Mia looked offended as though I was completely out of line, thank you very much. "Oh, the Guatemalan princess doesn't want to be scolded," Mary would observe after I'd told Mia that "we" don't throw food from the high chair or pull our sister's hair. In response Mia leaned away from me, raised her chin, and regarded me evenly.

"Your Majesty," I sometimes said, "such behavior is beneath you."

We would then take turns covering Mia's face with kisses.

As my new daughter's confidence began to grow, something switched in her. Instead of behaving almost regally, she seemed to realize that she actually was home. That she was not a guest but truly a member of the family. She began to disobey more, complain more, and test limits. When she was overtired, she arched her back and refused to be put down. Sometimes she launched into a long rant and it sounded to me like someone was telling me off in Spanish. (Actually, someone was!)

I knew I would have to discipline this little girl, but would I be compromising our bond if I punished her so soon after her homecoming?

This was getting very tricky.

12

Post-Adoption Blues

I felt like I had been through a sort of trauma by the time Mia got home. I worried that I had let David and the older kids down the many times I had been distracted or prone to sadness over the months. The self-confidence that I'd enjoyed as a young mom seemed to have been scraped away. I no longer knew what was going to happen next. In fact, I couldn't even guess. Would Mia adjust beautifully? Would she and I prove to the world (and to the adoption naysayers in our life) that she was meant to be a part of our family?

I didn't know how to deal with her recent spurts of misbehavior. She wasn't truly naughty, but our wires got crossed many times. I thought she meant one thing when she meant another. I would interpret a look or something she did as being defiant but later understood that she had meant nothing by it. Was I equipped to be a good mother to her?

On the bright side, all four children seemed to be transitioning well. The three older kids were patient when I had to sit quietly by Mia's crib to get her to sleep at naptime and at bedtime. They giggled with her in shared tubs and dressed her in plastic knight's armor and football helmets when they played in the basement together. They had fallen in love—and so had she.

It was me who, increasingly, didn't know which end was up.

Sometimes Isabel approached me when Mia was sitting on my lap. When her sister was close by, Mia would extend her arm and push her away, as if to say, "Your presence is not required."

She was the Guatemalan princess again, imperial and commanding. I'd laugh it off and tell Isabel that it was normal for newly adopted kids to act this way. "She just wants to make sure I'm *really* her mama," I said. Isabel usually handled these times with aplomb—or seemed to, anyway.

She seemed proud of Mia. More than once I heard her brag to a friend, "My sister is black. Like Mulan and Pocahontas." She said the word *black* as if she was talking about a designer fragrance or a cake, just out of the oven. It was luxurious.

"Mia's hair is black too," Isabel once said. "Like licorice."

"And I want to eat her up," I said, pretending to nibble on Mia's arm. The girls started laughing. "Eat me up, eat me up," Isabel shouted.

Before I had children, I thought adults who spoke of "eating children up" had lost their minds. People who, until uttering those words, had seemed quite reasonable suddenly sounded like merry cannibals before a feast. "I could just eat her up!" they'd shout, tracing the folds of fat around a baby's wrist. It creeped me out.

But I found myself engaging in food analogies after Mia got home. Hair like licorice. Skin like coffee. Or caramel. Or chocolate. Or brown sugar.

She was, I had to admit, quite delicious.

In my mind I'd spent the last several months growing my relationship with Isabel, putting money in the bank, as it were, by all the quantity *and* quality time we had shared. But that wasn't the way my three-year-old's economy worked. Sharing her mama with another child, being pushed away and standing back while family, friends, and even strangers *oohed* and *aahed* over Mia had to be exceedingly difficult for her. And now this eating-her-up business.

That summer our family often walked down the street to the field at the middle school. Some of us played baseball, Isabel either rode her tricycle or made chalk drawings on the pavement, and Mia practiced walking or played games with her sister. One evening, I told David I'd clean the kitchen after our early dinner, get the girls washed up, and then join him and the boys at the field. The girls and I chatted as I loaded the dishwasher. Before we left, I laid Mia on the carpet to check her diaper. I remember I was singing something to her, maybe the ABCs, in my efforts to bring her up to speed on American toddlerhood.

Isabel had been sitting on the edge of the couch, but she suddenly got up and walked to where I crouched, still bending over Mia.

"You," she said, pointing at the middle of my chest. "You are a bad person and a bad mother."

"What?" I was stunned. "Honey, what?"

She turned and walked to the window, her back to me.

I understand now that this was a very little girl's attempt to let me know how hurt she felt. After being the youngest child in the family, the only girl, and the object of so much affection and admiration, suddenly someone else was getting all the attention. Mia was the focus of every person we passed on the street or at the park on in the grocery store. People dropped by throughout the summer and brought Mia gifts of clothes and toys. It was Christmas every day for her.

Mia had also begun to push her away more frequently. "My," she would say when Isabel started to climb up on my lap.

"Mia," I would say sternly. "I'm your mama *and* Isabel's mama. You can both sit on my lap."

"My," she would repeat, pushing Isabel away.

No wonder Isabel was hurt.

You are a bad person and a bad mother. It was such an unexpected, unusual thing for her to say. Before and after that moment, Isabel has been one of my most devoted fans. She's the girl who, on seeing me check my lipstick or brush my hair before leaving the house, winds her arms around me and says, "You're beautiful, Mom." She praises the food I make, the presents I give her, and the work I do. At eleven, as was true when she was two years old, she still often comes up close to me and whispers, "You're my best friend."

But that day, her words crippled me. It felt like someone had reached into my chest and crumpled up my heart the way you might ball up a letter bearing bad news. I finished changing Mia's diaper and then took the girls downstairs to the basement. My legs felt hollow, almost as if I were walking on a layer of air. I silently put a videotape in the player for them. *Kipper*, maybe, or *Caillou*. I walked up the stairs, closed the door to my room, and lay down on my bed. For the next hour, I could not stop crying.

What had I done?

What had become of that confident mom who always knew how to handle her children?

Was I both a bad person *and* a bad mother?

My own daughter had said so.

I cried until the movie ended and the girls, now snuggling on the big red couch in the basement and giggling with each other, yelled to say, "It's over!"

The refrain of my children's preschool years. "Mo-om," shouted in two syllables, "it's oh-ver."

I told them I was coming down, washed my face, went down the steps into the basement, and put a new tape in.

When my husband returned home later with the boys, he seemed annoyed. "Where were you? I thought you said you were going to walk down." Then he saw my swollen eyes.

At church that week I told a friend what had happened.

"Oh, it makes perfect sense," she said. "Isabel just said the two things that would hurt you the most. She knows you. She knows you want to be a good mom and a good person. She's just hurting and is too little to be able to tell you."

That day wasn't the last time I closed myself into my room to cry.

Why was this happening? Why couldn't three-year-old Isabel just "use her words" and clearly explain the various ways her sister's homecoming had affected her? Why couldn't Mia see that I really, really needed her to buck up and get with the system? No more contrariness. No more of this possessive behavior. No throwing food off the high chair. No screaming in her crib.

In retrospect, what they were going through could not have been more normal. But at the time, it felt like the end of the world. Somehow, just as Mia hit seventeen or eighteen months, I conveniently forgot that I'd always found that period—from about eighteen to twenty-four months—the most difficult one as a parent. At that age, children are in-between. They want to do more than their bodies allow. They long for freedom. They are frustrated by their inability to express themselves clearly. Add to that the incredible changes she was dealing with and someone should have given Mia the Medal of Honor for her bravery and good humor.

● ● ●

Years later, I spoke about that difficult time to a women's group. It was an intergenerational crowd; our ages ranged from about thirty to eighty years old. We had gathered to talk about raising children. Some of the women were adoptive mothers. Others were interested in learning more about adoption. A few wanted to hear more details about families with children by birth and by adoption.

We drank coffee out of the miscellaneous mugs that can be found in church kitchen cabinets. Clear glass, bone china, solid ceramic mugs with the names of long-forgotten conferences printed on them. Some of us attend the church in whose library we met. (*Library* is too grand a name for the room, but one wall is indeed lined with bookshelves holding books.)

Starting when Theo was a newborn, and then for several years, I sat in that very same room every other week as a part of a mothers' group. We drank from the stained mugs. We held babies on our laps. We fumbled in our bags for pacifiers or blocks or crayons. We had dark circles under our eyes and an aching hunger for adult company.

We knew the early months of caring for a baby to be sometimes isolating and, concurrently, sometimes so full of wonder the world seemed to be splitting apart and beginning anew. It was good to get out of the house and talk to other people in the same moment in life. I never checked a book out of that library, but I left that room recharged every time I was there.

I imagined I'd be sitting in that room every month until I was, like some of the mothers, the parent of teenagers or college students. I saw us all going gray together and following each other's stories in a long, unbroken narrative. But, as always, things change. My friend Andrea, who first welcomed me to the group, moved from Chicago to Washington State. Since then, her old house, a Cape Cod not far from mine, has twice been listed for sale. Both times I've called her, wishing that we could go back in time. "Your house is for sale again. Couldn't you just move back?"

Also, my children began school, and so instead of toting them along with me to the grocery store or mothers' group, my life shifted toward getting them to the places they needed to be. I started to miss the group once in a while and then more often. Sometimes just folding a big mound of laundry took precedence over going. I changed from being a parent who carefully consulted the baby books before introducing pureed carrots to someone who realized that there was only so much I could know about these little ones and how to care for them. After Mia's adoption, I stayed close to home for a while. Just when I probably should have been part of a vital mothers' group, I drew back, disappointed in myself, worried on some level at least that I was a "bad mom and a bad person." I was busier, less confident. In short, things got more complicated.

The mothers' group changed dramatically. More members moved. Others found themselves often too busy to go. That library, once a sanctuary for me in somehow just as real a way as the nave with its pews and altar, became just a passageway on

Sunday mornings. There were the books I'd never check out. There were the diamond-shaped panes of color in the stained-glass windows. It was just a strange old room with institutional tables and a mishmash of old mugs on a side table.

But then, years after I'd left it, I found myself there again to talk about parenting and adoption. Things had changed. There were no babies in attendance. Several of the women had gray hair. And, instead of sharing the previous night's misadventures with baby or details about visiting the pediatrician, the conversation arched back over decades. Two older women told stories about their children's adoptions. They acknowledged that, long ago, secrecy shrouded adoption. They all agreed that this was damaging not only to their children but also to their children's birthparents and to themselves. "It was just the way it was done," one said. "We were told it was the best way." One woman's adult son finally expressed the pain of trying to understand why his birthparents placed him for adoption, many years after he'd left home. With the benefit of years, these women summarized large chunks of time and saw the way wounds healed only after secrets were exposed.

Sitting in that room again, I couldn't help but reflect on all that changed in my life since the time I was a regular member of the mothers' group. Shadows of old conversations and friendships lingered in the corners. While I felt their absence, I also felt the vitality of the women who now sat around me at the table—their honesty, strength, and the wealth of wisdom they possess.

When I brought Theo to that mothers' group when he was only weeks old, I had no idea that only seven years later I'd be the mother of four. I didn't know what kind of parent I'd be. I didn't know that one of my children would come to us by adoption, opening my family's world to another culture, another country, and another family's family tree. I couldn't have foreseen that adopting my daughter would require her to experience a very real loss and that this loss would remain with her, and with me.

Sometimes that loss would be as innocuous as a book on a shelf, sometimes as heartening as a conversation among old friends, and sometimes as violent as a crash of lightning.

● ● ●

When I was a little girl, I loved watching movies on television in our basement family room. Remember *The Boy in the Plastic Bubble*? I even loved old war movies like *Sink the Bismarck* on Family Classics. I would lose myself in after-school specials with their not-so-subtle warnings about using drugs, hitchhiking, or other societal ills. Whatever the story, I couldn't help but get drawn in, almost from the start. I'd begin to care about the characters and believe in the world of the story.

But then—it happened. ("It" always happened.) Some dose of bad luck would rain down on the character. My stomach would tie up in knots and, as the conflict raged, I looked at books, picked at a worn spot on the sofa, or studied the frayed ends of my shoelaces. I was waiting for things to be cleared up and for everyone to be happy again. I still find myself standing, clearing the discarded juice boxes or popcorn kernels in the truly difficult parts of movies. "No, no. It's okay. Don't pause it. I can hear from the kitchen . . ."

I would find out later that screenplays are written in three acts. The first act tells who the film is about, where it takes place, and what is going to happen. The second act is when the main character encounters a series of obstacles. It's in the last act when our hearts slow down to a normal pace. All is again right with the world—or, at least, some resolution has occurred.

I rarely see that three-act structure in life. In terms of the adoption process, the decision period could be framed as the first act. The camera could linger on my three older kids playing on the driveway on a spring day. One would teeter on rollerblades, another draw with sidewalk chalk, and the third would heave a basketball toward the backboard. Another scene in this act could be my husband, calling home from a business trip to India, telling me about the street children who stood on the highway median and knocked on the windows of his car. Next, you could see us sitting excitedly across from our social worker at the adoption agency, then photocopying documents, and, lastly, buying a bunk bed for our daughters' room.

In the second act the obstacles come. Months could be shown passing, maybe like they did in old movies, with pages, each representing a day, flying off the calendar. The camera could show the empty crib. Summer would turn to fall. The sky would be darker. There would be tears, anguished conversations, and scattered pictures of Mia in Guatemala.

The third act would be the joyous one. It would be spring again. David and I fly home from Guatemala City. My new daughter is on my lap. She drinks water through a straw. She giggles with delight at the board books I read to her.

But Mia's homecoming wasn't the end; it was only the beginning of the story. What followed didn't seem to fit a predictable story-structure. If it were filmed, there would be scenes of my holding her closely. Others with me shaking my finger at her as she sat on the bottom stair in a time-out. There would be shots of her siblings feeding her, giving her hugs, or glaring at her after she had pulled a toy out of their hands.

I don't know why I thought having a child who was adopted would be any different than raising the children to whom I gave birth. Sometimes one of my four kids rubs me the wrong way, is cranky, or behaves unfairly to his siblings. Other days, my love for that same one almost knocks me flat and I feel like the most fortunate person in the world. But, mostly, I live away from those extremes in the rhythms of everyday family life.

Not all adoptions end happily. Some leave the parents feeling diminished and regretful. A few "disrupt" or are legally dissolved. Older ages and existing emotional and behavioral problems— often stemming from abuse or neglect in early life—seem to be the factors that can make disruption more likely. I don't know why good people, whose intentions to adopt were borne of love, have to face such pain. It would take a compassionate theologian or philosopher to address those questions, and I am neither.

What I do know is that—much as I hated it when I was a little girl—all our life stories contain some measure of grief and challenge and there are no guarantees that one's family, marriage, career, or friendships will play out in a predictable, three-act structure.

● ● ●

Some evenings, while the older kids shower and finish their homework, I help Mia in the bath. After lathering her hair, scrubbing her dirty feet, and hiding the little wind-up diver under a mountain of bubbles for the umpteenth time, the time comes to rinse her off and get her to bed. She stands, knee-deep in bubbles, as I take down the shower nozzle and test the temperature. "Look up at the ceiling," I say as I begin to rinse her head. She stands still as I rinse her and then she steps out on the bath mat, all the while telling me about the game she played with a friend at recess that day.

Her bath times were not always so easy. For her first few years home, she panicked when the water hit her head and body. She'd stomp and scream and I would hold her awkwardly—getting soaked myself—so that she wouldn't slip in the bathtub. Other times I'd fill a plastic container with clean water to rinse her hair. Same routine—shrieking and panic. Lying down in the tub to rinse her wasn't an option—this elicited even more horror than the shower nozzle.

I was fairly tolerant of such episodes for the first few months after her adoption. I was aware that her world looked, smelled, and sounded completely different than the one she knew for the first year and a half of her life. We were still bonding.

But as months passed, my patience would run low. Sometimes I lost my temper and handled her like an industrious health-care worker, not attempting to placate or speak to her but just getting the job done quickly and efficiently. Sometimes I would plead with her, beginning when she probably couldn't yet understand much of what I said. "It's okay. We'll be done soon. I won't hurt you!"

Again I second-guessed myself, wondered whether I was cut out to be a mother. I wished that Mia could see into my heart and know that I could be trusted. But trust takes time.

It took more than months to build complete trust; it took years. Only after about three or four years after her homecoming, Mia awarded me with the same easy trust that my other kids do.

She lets me do hasty nose clean-ups outside school before taking her inside. She lets me clean her ears, trim her nails, lop off the ends of her bangs, and, of course, bathe her. And, all the while, she chatters away to me about her day or the dog or whatever else she is thinking.

When Mark and Mary were adopting from China years ago, they were told by their agency that it takes children twice as long as they were in their original homes to adjust to their new ones. So if you adopt a child at four months old, it will be at least eight months before she is attached and adjusted. When Mark and Mary told me this, I bristled at the idea. I'd witnessed the love that flowed between their new baby and them from the moment they walked through the sliding doors into O'Hare's baggage area. Twice as long as she was in China until she was bonded and adjusted? No way!

But now I think the caseworker was right.

In my relationship with Mia, although we had affection and bonding from the time we said good-bye to her foster mother and rode the elevator up to our hotel room in Guatemala City, trust took time to build.

13

Tummy Ladies and Other Kinds of Mothers

September 2003

Dear Friends,

Today was Mia's re-adoption day. We appeared in court in Chicago to adopt her under Illinois law. It wasn't a requirement, but a means by which her paperwork (including her birth certificate) will be condensed and made more user-friendly for her as she goes through life in the US. We took Ian and Isabel with us to appear before the judge. Sadly, Isabel killed any chance she had for a political career when she perjured herself. After raising her right hand and swearing to tell the truth, she told the judge that she goes to preschool on Mondays and Fridays when indeed it's Tuesdays and Thursday mornings. Oh well. Now she'll never be president. (The perjury thing is bound to come out. Such scandals always do, right?)

It surprised me that today felt more like her adoption day

than when we were given her documents at the US embassy in Guatemala City or when we brought her home. Now we know her, we were in a familiar place, and it all was finally . . . final.

We are so blessed that she is our daughter, little mystery and gift that she is.

Love from,

Jen

As I got more rest and our family life settled down, my confidence began to recover and grow.

As I told a friend, after Mia's adoption I felt like her mother but not her *adoptive* mother. As time passed, however, I began to bump into adoption issues such as race and questions about her past. I was reminded that although my heart knew I was her real mother, it was also true that I was her mother by adoption.

● ● ●

My husband is color-blind. When it comes up in conversation, he'll quickly attempt to dodge the label. "No, I just have some trouble with greens and reds," he says, meekly.

No one likes being put in a box, right?

But he inadvertently reveals the severity of his problem more often than he knows. In a roomful of people, David might ask, "Who's that guy in the gray hat?" I'll look around for a while before I remember that, in my eyes, there may be no one at all who is wearing a gray hat.

I learned about his color-blindness not long after we were engaged. One autumn day, David and I scrunched around the blanket of fallen leaves on our college campus, collecting the most beautiful ones we could find. The leaves I gathered were vibrant reds and yellows. The way I saw it, all of David's were brown. Brown like a discarded paper sack.

"Hey! Look at this one!" he'd shout, waving another brown leaf at me.

"Wow. Yeah," I said. (I was trying to be supportive.)

Over the years, I've thought how interesting it is that two people can look at the same thing—a red leaf, say, or a brown one—but see it so differently from the other. It sometimes makes me think about race. When people see Mia—that chocolatey skin and hair as black as licorice—I wonder what they see.

Now that my family is multiethnic (or transracial or whatever you like to call it), my views on race have changed. I've learned that race does, in fact, matter. I've learned that even when they insist they are, people are not color-blind. (Other than those who suffer from it in the traditional way, like David.) I have come to see that for people who aren't white in our culture, race is a defining element of life. Being white is a ticket or membership pass; being a person of color is a strike.

I used to think talking about race was passé, uninteresting, and no longer relevant, but now that I'm the mother of a child "of color," my vision has changed. Waiting outside our daughters' gymnastics class, two other mothers and I chat pleasantly about the program. Someone asks where to find a certain kind of leotard. Someone else wonders when registration for the next session will begin. When class is over and the lobby fills with boys and girls looking for their mothers, one of the moms I've been chatting with bends to greet two blonde girls who have just knocked into her.

"Oh here you are, darling," she says. "Did you have fun today?"

She straightens herself up and turns to find Mia standing in front of her. The smile disappears from her face.

"Excuse me," she says in a voice so cold that others stop and look.

"Hi, sweetie," I almost shout. "Over here!"

The woman sees that Mia is my daughter and attempts to smile. "Oh . . . she," she mumbles.

For now, Mia seems blissfully unaware that when some people see her, they can't get past the color of her skin. Or maybe it's not about color, but about perceived class. When I hear people make offhand or patronizing comments about the Hispanic men who mow their lawn, or imitate the Spanish accent of the person clearing tables at a restaurant, I think, *Is that what you see when you see my beautiful daughter?*

It reminds me to keep saying those words from the prayer book, asking God to help me "respect the dignity of every person." The dignity, worthiness, and excellence of every single person.

● ● ●

"I love seeing your kids," a woman named Jackie once said to me, long before Mia came home. We were leaving the park just as she and her kids were arriving. "They always look like they've been having fun. They're a mess, like mine." I remember glancing down at Ian and Isabel in their stroller. Ian's hair was matted down with sweat and he wore sand on his hands like gloves. Isabel's hair was a tangle of curls and her face was stained from a Popsicle from the ice cream truck. (As I mentioned before, I didn't maintain the pears and brie dessert tradition. Once it was discovered that Oreos were "always available," our dessert menu changed radically.)

"Yep," I laughed. "We can always take 'em home and hose 'em off, right?"

"That's right," she said.

I'm sure I bathed them both that day, likely after stopping at the grocery store or library.

I wasn't as comfortable, however, taking Mia out when she was sticky or grass-stained. I didn't want her to be judged. Had she just gotten filthy at the park, I would have scrubbed her down once I got home and dressed her in clean clothes.

Perhaps that is part of what it means to be a conspicuous family, the way we try to protect our children from the judgment of others.

As Mia got a bit older, she began noticing her racial difference. "I no like my arms," she said one day. "I like Iz-bel's arms."

She rubbed her forearms. They were darkly tanned from the sun.

"Oh, honey," I said. "You are beautiful. You are exactly the way God wanted you to be. Brown and lovely and beautiful."

I started making observations to the kids, as we drove around town, about the tanning spas we passed. I tried to pass these remarks off as health warnings. "Hm . . . you know the light used in tanning beds is very dangerous. It causes cancer."

Isabel would fall right into my trap.

"But then why do people go there?"

"Great question, Isabel! Well, you see, some people want to make their skin darker. They might be fair-skinned like Mommy, but want to look dark, like, say . . . Mia."

"Do you want to go there?" Mia asked.

"No. To be honest, when I was a teenager sometimes I thought about making my skin browner." (I refrained from sharing the embarrassing story of my complete failure as a sunbather.) "But now I like the way I look. I'm meant to be this color."

I noticed, as time went on, that Mia seemed more comfortable with her brown skin. In careful self-portraits, she colored her face and arms brown.

"Beautiful," I said.

She smiled and nodded, and I would go review my stack of adoption books to make sure I wasn't forgetting to say something essential in this conversation.

● ● ●

"Ruby don't like lions," Mia announced one day. Ruby is Mark and Mary's second child and, since that first vacation in South Dakota years ago, Mia's best friend. Ruby and Mia are nearly the same age. Ruby, however, was born in China and came home with Mark and Mary several months before Mia's adoption was finalized. The two of them were fast friends, two open-hearted, black-haired girls who march through life with palpable solidarity. They were in the same preschool class and they are always begging for play dates, ever eager to run off into the basement and dress as princesses or pirates or knights or, usually, some combination of the three.

From the time Mia was able to speak, she has liked to chat about Ruby. She tells me what Ruby does and does not like or funny things Ruby has told her about school or her sisters. Mia is a professional Ruby expert and still sometimes proclaims—apropos of nothing—that Ruby does or does not like a certain flavor of ice cream or style of bathing suit.

When Mia was about three, she liked to talk about the details of Ruby's birth. Maybe she was curious about her own early life or maybe it was just another excuse to talk about her favorite person.

"Ruby was borned in China," she said to me one day. "Aunt Mary went to China and Ruby came out of her tummy and then they came home. Babies grow in mommies' tummies and then they bust out the belly button."

"Well they don't exactly get born that way, but you're right that Ruby was born in China," I said. "But her Mommy and Daddy went to China to adopt her, just like Daddy and I adopted you."

Mia shrugged dismissively and ate another spoonful of macaroni and cheese.

My mind starting flipping through the pages of a book I'd read during the adoption process. It was a book I suddenly realized I needed to read again. The book is *Talking to Young Children About Adoption* by Mary Watkins and Susan Fisher.[1] Sitting across the table from my daughter, I realized that when I first read it, my focus wasn't on the information the authors set out to impart. Instead, while reading the anecdotes of mothers talking to their adopted children about their origins, I was hungry to get a peek at the intimate portrayals of parent/child relationships.

When I first read the book, Mia still lived with Maria in Guatemala. I had witnessed their affectionate relationship on our trip there and had to wonder whether Mia and I would ever share such tenderness. Mia stroked Maria's hair, nuzzled her when she was sleepy, and buried her head against her shoulder. As I read the book, I hopped around the chapters, looking for clues. Did the young kids resent their mothers for taking them from their native countries? Did children understand their mothers' deep love? Did they share the same kind of closeness that I had with my three older children? Skimming through the book, I felt affirmed. These relationships were healthy, open, and warm. Reading it gave me a sense that everything was going to be all right. But I skimmed over too much of it and, as Mia spoke about Ruby's birth, I silently chastised myself for being such a poor student.

"Ruby's mommy went far, far away to pick her up. Like you picked me up," Mia said, turning the idea over in her mind.

"That's right. And Ruby's mommy and daddy were so happy, just like Daddy and I were. They wanted her for their daughter so much!"

"Ruby didn't come out of her mommy's tummy button," Mia said, staring at me intently. "Ruby didn't get borned out a tummy."

"*All* babies come out of women's tummies, but Ruby didn't come out of her mommy's tummy. Not Mary's. She came from another woman's tummy. Sometimes a woman can't take care of her baby because she is poor or sick. So then when the baby is born, someone else gets to take care of the baby and be the mommy," I said.

"Did I come from Maria's tummy?" my daughter asked.

"No, honey. Maria was like a babysitter. She took care of you after you were born until we could come and bring you home, but you didn't come out of her tummy."

"She was my babysitter," she said thoughtfully. But then, alarmed, asked, "What tummy did I come out?"

Ooh. The big question. I took a breath and looked her in the eyes.

In *Talking to Young Children About Adoption*, the authors

suggest that using the word "mother" in multiple ways ("birth-mother," "foster mother," "adoptive mother") can be confusing to very young children. To a young child, there is only one "Mommy." They employ the term "tummy lady" to describe the birthmother.

"Your tummy lady was someone else, not Maria. She is a kind person in Guatemala but she was very poor and wanted you to be safe and happy, so Mommy and Daddy adopted you—"

"And you were so, so happy!" she said.

"We were the happiest people in the whole world because we love you higher than mountains."

"There are mountains in Guatemala," Mia noted.

"Yes," I said, relieved that this first foray into the topic of her birthmother didn't seem to upset her. I knew there would be other, much more difficult conversations in the future, but at least we were off to a good start.

"Ruby don't like mountains," Mia said, scraping the bottom of her bowl with her spoon. "Can I have dessert now?"

● ● ●

On a chilly night, Mia and I were left alone for the evening. My husband had taken the three older children to an event at their school that ended well past her bedtime. I'd promoted the evening to her all day in an effort to reduce her disappointment about not going with the others.

"We'll have a special time together. You and me. Just the two of us."

She picked her favorite library book from the stack. I read to her, aware of the time passing, eyeing the clock as it crept toward seven o'clock when I'd take her upstairs to get ready for bed. It had been a tiring few weeks—I wanted to go to bed early myself.

"I want to see her," Mia said.

Her comment pulled me back into the moment. *See her?* The book we were reading was about a little white terrier named Fergus. In one illustration, he stares at his owner during dinner, putting a paw on the man's leg to indicate a desire for scraps. We had just been laughing at the picture that follows that one—Fergus's face smeared orange, with bits of spaghetti clinging to his fur.

"See who?" I asked.

Mia turned around in my lap and looked in my eyes.

"I want to see the lady whose tummy I came out of."

I closed the book.

When Mia was eight months old, she sat on the edge of her birthmother's lap for a photograph. That morning, both of them had their blood taken so that their biological relationship could be confirmed. We had photocopies of that picture. The moment I first saw it, before even meeting Mia, I knew it was one of the most important pieces of paper I owned.

I'd last mentioned the picture to Mia several months before that night. We had been talking about how babies grow inside their mothers' bodies.

"Theo came out of your tummy," she said.

"Yes, he did."

"Isabel came out of your tummy."

"Yes, she did."

"Ian came out of your tummy."

"Yes."

"But I came from someone else's tummy."

"Yes," I'd said, "and we have a picture of her. If you ever want to see it, I can show it to you." That night she hadn't asked.

"I want to see that picture," Mia said, still looking in my eyes.

I left her on the chair and found the firebox that contains all the documents related to her adoption. There it was. The cover sheet was from a lab in the United States and stated that maternity had been established. On the next page, the photographs.

I stared again at the unfamiliar woman holding her little baby, a baby she hadn't seen for several months. Her brows are drawn together; a deep crease divides her forehead. I brought the papers upstairs, sat again in the chair, and lifted my daughter onto my lap. I held the page in front of her and she looked at it, silently, for a very long time.

"I miss her so much," she said, beginning to cry. I pulled her close to me and told her it was all right. She hugged me and then turned again to the page, eyes locking on the image.

She told me that she was confused when they took the picture. "I didn't know what was going on," she said, studying her baby self in the photo.

We talked about the circumstances her birthmother faced and the hopes she had for Mia. Later in the evening, I made a photocopy of that piece of paper, cut out the image, and put it in a frame. She ran upstairs and put the frame beside her bed, the picture facing her pillow.

● ● ●

Every May, we celebrate Mia's homecoming anniversary. It's the day my husband and I signed the final set of papers that made us her parents at the US embassy in Guatemala City. Some adoptive parents call this day "Gotcha Day." I have nothing against the name, but it's not one I use. I have an unfortunate tendency to roll things over and over in my mind and for me, that term fails to acknowledge the ambivalence that I felt related to my daughter's adoption. Amid the joy of bringing her to our family and the confidence that this was just the child for us, my thoughts would linger on the losses—of culture, of language, of proximity to her biological family—that she unknowingly experienced when we brought her home. I think of her birthmother and the poverty she endures.

So I just refer to this special day as her "homecoming anniversary." Some years, we celebrate only by talking about it over dinner and telling the story of bringing her home. Other years we make a bigger deal of it. The older kids write Mia notes telling her what she means to them or what they remember about her homecoming. We play music, have a special meal, and one year, my bigger kids even adorned themselves with washable tattoos of hearts and letters that spelled out their sister's name. Some years I almost forget about Mia's homecoming anniversary. It feels like she's been home forever and the fact of her adoption isn't the first thing on my mind when I think of her. The flurry of "adoptive issues" that I addressed in her first few years home have retreated.

But when she was first home, they often seemed more common.

When Mia was approaching three years old and we were at yet another of the countless dentist appointments that were required to fill the seventeen or so cavities she came home with, the hygienist looked up at me warily.

Mia was reclined in the dentist's chair, wearing a pair of orange-framed sunglasses to shield her eyes from the bright light.

"So . . . have you talked to anyone about her speech problem?" the hygienist asked. I could tell she had decided that she might be giving me this news for the first time but would pretend like it was so obvious that it likely was already on my mind. She was well meaning and asked her question confidently to help me save face, but really I just felt insulted.

"I have an appointment to have her evaluated," I said.

The hygienist smiled and nodded. She seemed pleased to have correctly tagged my daughter's problem.

But for Pete's sake, how could I not have noticed? Even when others seemed bewildered by what Mia was saying, I could understand her. Many parents of young children find themselves in the role of translator from time to time. If you spend enough time with a child, you learn their unique language. I was just sorry that other people couldn't enjoy her funny observations. I worried about how it must feel to her to have grown-ups bending down to her, their faces screwed up in a frown, and then asking me, "What did she say?"

I felt aggravated, too, that her speech problem was so evident that everyone from the dental hygienist to the bagger at the grocery store was offering unsolicited advice. Of course they were right, but as the person who spent her days interacting with Mia, it felt patronizing. And would they have chimed in with advice if she were not so obviously a child who was adopted?

Yes, yes, I know! She's difficult to understand!

The problem filled me with anxiety. What was causing these problems? Were her mouth and tongue shaped well for speech? Was it that she spent the first almost year and a half of her life in Guatemala, learning and listening to Spanish phrases before suddenly being thrown into an English-speaking world? Was it that she is the youngest of four and the older kids rapidly responded to her gestures and grunts toward a certain toy or food? Was it that I was speaking too quickly to her? Would she have had speech problems in her native language too?

Whatever the causes, by the time she was about two and a half, I knew she would likely need speech therapy. I called a local pre-school that serves kids with special needs and was told that they didn't evaluate kids until after they turned three years old. I put the appointment on the calendar and waited, trying to enunciate as clearly as possible when I read her books or gave her instructions.

"*Goodnight Moon*," I read. My *moon*'s elongated "n" pulled my face into a smile. My pronunciation of the "t" in *goodnight* was as crisp as toast. I sounded like I was narrating a documentary on, I don't know, rare birds of the Galápagos Islands on PBS. ("*Regard the sharp-beaked ground finch in all its glory . . .*")

Mia's third birthday approached and with it the appointment at the preschool. As the day drew nearer, I was apprehensive about the evaluation. Would my daughter have lifelong speech problems? Would she require surgery for a problem with her hard palate? What other problems—emotional or physical—might be identified? When the morning of our appointment finally came, however, my spirit was calmed soon after we entered the building. The staff treated us gently, and my daughter was immediately at ease. Together with a few other children and their parents, we played in a room as school staff members observed us and, later, joined into our play. Then the children went off on their own with the "teachers" (a social worker, preschool teacher, nurse, and speech therapist among them) to interact. About an hour and a half later, my daughter returned.

The following week I received a phone call from the school saying that they recommended speech therapy for my daughter. I was told that I would receive a full report regarding her social, emotional, behavioral, and developmental progress in the next day or two. I hungrily watched for the envelope and when it came I tore it open. Reading the charts and notes, I felt the kind of glee a person might have when she's been admitted into college or finds that she is being promoted.

At this preschool, whose staff were accustomed to seeing kids with a wide range of abilities and special needs, Mia didn't seem different. In fact, no one was tagged as "different" there, but all children were viewed as the complex, unique people they are. Some had challenges, to be sure, but there didn't seem to be a firm definition of what a "normal" three-year-old was like. Mia had a problem saying her "s" sounds. She was emotionally secure. The social worker made positive comments about our mother-daughter free play. The report meant a lot to me and quieted many of my adoptive-mother fears. We hadn't completely traumatized her by taking her from her native culture.

Mia started speech therapy at our local elementary school. It was close by. It was free. It was familiar to her after tagging along with me to various volunteer tasks there.

After our first meeting I wrote the speech therapist a quick note confirming our next appointment and telling her a bit more about Mia's story.

May 2005

It was good to meet you this morning. Thanks for your help with Mia. She told me on the way home that she liked you and that she was a little bit scared at first. She tends to get quiet and a bit poker-faced when she is frightened or in a new place. After we met, I saw the nurse for the recommended hearing test. She passed. I don't know whether this has anything to do with her speech issues, but Mia came home from Guatemala, where she was born, about two years ago. She lived there for the first sixteen months of her life and had only heard Spanish spoken during that time. After her adoption, she spoke some Spanish to us—just a word here or there but clearly understood a lot of Spanish. Her post-adoption physical was done in Spanish by a doctor who speaks it fluently and Mia responded to all of his requests ("open your mouth," etc.).

After she was home for a little over a month, she stopped speaking entirely. When she spoke again a month later, she only spoke in English. When Spanish speakers (the same doctor, a church nursery helper, etc.) spoke to her in Spanish, it was obvious that she had no idea what was being said to her. I don't know whether that's got anything to do with her speech problem, but I thought you might want to know.

Best,

Jennifer

Mia's speech therapist was a wonder. She created games, crafts, and activities for Mia to do every week. Isabel was in afternoon kindergarten at that time and sat with Mia and me in the speech therapist's office those mornings, drawing or looking at books. Mia loved "learning her sounds" and, had she needed it, she could have continued speech therapy when she began kindergarten at the school. After a year, however, she passed out of the district's special education program.

I took special pleasure in hearing her chat with strangers at the grocery store or park.

No more bewildered faces.

No more need for translation.

14

Her Story

A full moon. A hurried drive to the hospital on a rainy night. The way he stared at us. How she rushed into the world, raging at the bright lights and cold of the delivery room. The glint of delight in his eyes. My three older children love to hear the stories of their births. We laugh in recognition about the way their newborn selves foretold the people they would be—his focus, her spirit, his joyfulness.

Of course, I can't tell these kinds of stories to Mia; I wasn't there.

After her adoption, David and I sometimes jokingly enumerated the benefits of having adopted a toddler. I was glad to avoid the heartburn, weight gain, and other indignities of pregnancy. He liked lopping off a year of diaper changes and skipping those frequent middle-of-the-night feedings that infants require. Indeed, in our case adopting a toddler meant bringing home a child who let us know when she was hungry, who slept through the night, and who laughed and played with her older siblings right from the start.

And yet, those benefits only tell a sliver of the story. I would trade anything I own to have experienced my youngest child's first months. To be the one who coaxed out her first smile. To have watched her mouth pucker at a first bite of applesauce from a tiny spoon. To have been her constant companion since birth, inadvertently building her trust day by day. But that is not our story. Like all adopted children, there is a part of my daughter's history that we do not share.

Experts recommend that adoptive parents find ways to tell children, from as young as possible, as much about their pre-adoption lives as possible. One way to do this is to create a Lifebook—basically a scrapbook that tells your adopted children as much as possible about the lives they led before coming home. Lifebooks can give internationally adopted children information on the countries of their birth. If details are known about the child's birth, these are included. Whereas a baby book tells the story of the family, a Lifebook tells an individual story of an adopted child. By recording the story of children's births and placements, we empower our children. We embrace and give them their story.

I made a Lifebook for Mia. Its pages are decorated with post-cards of Guatemala, photographs of her foster mother, and the infant pictures we received from our agency. I included copies of the letters I wrote to Maria when Mia was in her care and photo-graphs of the toys and clothing we sent to her. The text is a story, told from my daughter's perspective, that details what we know about her early life in Guatemala.

Before she could read it herself, I read her the Lifebook at least weekly. In her first year home, she would point animatedly at the photos of her foster mother. Later, she seemed to forget

Maria and quickly turned the pages to the ones that pictured David and me with her on that first visit to Guatemala. As a very little girl, she called it her "special book." Sometimes when we had guests, she whispered in my ear, "I want to show my special book." It was an honor she bestowed on people she liked and trusted. It was her way of saying, "I like you. I am going to tell you who I am."

Perhaps, then, the person would be able to "learn to know" her.

She knew from the start that she had a history distinct from anyone else in the family. A history that only she had experienced. And sometimes, as clever younger siblings do, she used that information to wield power. When they were three and five, my girls were watching an episode of *Bob the Builder* that featured porcupines. Mia turned to Isabel and said, "I touched a porcupine when I was in Guatemala."

Isabel protested, "No you didn't! They don't even *have* porcupines in Guatemala."

"Yes they do. I touched one," Mia insisted. "In Guatemala. Before you met me." It was her trump card.

In time, I took the book to a copy shop and made her a color copy with a laminated cover. She had begun taking her Lifebook with her—in the car, to her grandparents' houses, or in her backpack for preschool. I gave her the copy and put the original on a high shelf. I wanted to keep a pristine version of it for when she was older.

In the months preceding my daughter's homecoming, I became almost obsessed with creating a birth announcement for her. I looked at online stationery sites. I visited card shops and paged through their enormous books of samples. I kept a file of poetry, Bible verses, and other text that I might use. It seemed like a crucial task to me, making the nicest birth and adoption announcement anyone had ever received. Looking back, I believe it was one of the ways I dealt with missing her and with the knowledge that, unlike my older kids, no one had ever thrown a baby shower or a birthday party to celebrate her life. As soon as she was my girl, I wanted to do it right.

Tap, tap, tap. "Testing . . . testing. Attention, everyone! Yes, and I mean you over there, Belarus. You too, Lesotho—I haven't forgotten about you. Please pardon the delay, but I have an announcement for the whole world. A person of great worth and significance has entered human history. Without further ado, I present to you—my daughter!"

I finally accomplished my task and chose an announcement. It is pasted on page one of Mia's Lifebook. It is a square card bearing her name and her birth and adoption dates in raised, plum lettering. Its image is a lavender, watercolor crescent moon. At the bottom of the card, I quoted four lines from Joseph Addison's "Ode":

> *Soon as the evening shades prevail,*
> *The Moon takes up her wondrous tale,*
> *And nightly to the list'ning Earth,*
> *Repeats the story of her birth.*[1]

The first Sunday we were home with Mia, my family and I went to church. I admit I wasn't paying much attention to the liturgy or the hymns or the homily. I was caught up in the happiness of finally having my baby girl with me, snuggled against me in the sling. How many times had I restrained myself from tears on those Sunday mornings since the moment I got that little tap on the shoulder, telling me that another child was on the way? And here she was, wide-eyed and beautiful, sitting silently through the service.

The words of the final hymn that morning, chosen while our announcements were still waiting to be stamped and mailed, were from Joseph Addison's "Ode."

"Did you tell him? Did you tell Charles that we would be here and that I'd chosen those lines for Mia's announcement?" I asked David. He said he hadn't and that the choirmaster had likely chosen the hymn weeks ago, just because it related well to the Scripture readings. It was another affirmation. A little wave from God.

This is the story, with only a few private details excluded, that I wrote for Mia's Lifebook:

My name is Mia. I was born in February 2002 in the Central American country of Guatemala. Guatemala is the country just south of Mexico. Guatemala is a beautiful country. There are rugged mountains, rain forests, jungles, pine forests, volcanoes, and many rare and beautiful birds and other wildlife.

Guatemala is also the home of ancient Mayan temples and pyramids, and people come from all over the world to see them. The Mayan people first appeared in Guatemala more than 3,000 years ago.

Later, Spanish explorers came to Guatemala, and unfortunately they took over the land from the Indian people who lived there before them. Since that time, the indigenous, or first people, have not been treated very well in Guatemala.

Even before the Spanish people came to Guatemala, the

people there ate foods made from corn, including tortillas. Guatemalan people still eat a lot of corn and also eat rice and beans and other foods that are similar to what we find on the menu at a Mexican restaurant.

The Guatemalan people are very friendly people. They care very much about their families and celebrate many holidays. They also see the magic of the natural world, of birds and volcanoes and all of God's creation. They know how to relax and have fun. Although the official language of Guatemala is Spanish, more than twenty-seven other languages are spoken there.

Something very sad happened in Guatemala before I was born. The people who were Spanish and the people who were Indian had a terrible war. It lasted for thirty-six years which is a very, very long time. The war was, like all wars, a sad thing for everyone in the country. Many people were killed and the country was left very poor.

I was born only six years after the end of the war. The family that I was born into was very poor. The woman who gave birth to me worked very hard, but could not afford to give me the things I need to be healthy and happy. She cared about me and wanted me to have a good life. She decided that it would be best for me to join a different family outside of Guatemala. Many very poor women in Guatemala have to make the same choice when they have a baby.

God knew all about this, of course, and had already chosen my family even before my Mommy and Daddy were born. At the same time that I was being born in Guatemala, God was figuring out a way to let my Mommy and Daddy in America know that I would be coming along soon. When they found out that I was going to be a part of the family, they were so happy.

When I was a few days old, I went to live with a woman named Maria. Maria loved me very much and took very good care of me before my Mommy and Daddy were allowed to come to bring me home. It took several months for them to be able to come because lawyers in Guatemala and in the US had to do a lot of paperwork first.

When I was in Guatemala, Maria took me on walks in my stroller. I watched kids play basketball at the park. I ate all kinds of wonderful foods such as mangoes, watermelon, and squash. I even got to watch Barney on television!

Maria said I was the sweetest of all the sweet babies she ever cared for as a foster parent. But she knew all along that someday she would need to say good-bye and give me to my Mommy and Daddy. She loves God and knew that God had chosen my family for me, just like God does for all children everywhere.

While my Mommy and Daddy and my brothers, Theo and Ian, and my sister, Isabel, were waiting for the paperwork to be done in Guatemala, they got ready for me at home. They bought Isabel and me a bunk bed so when I got bigger we could share it. They put my crib into the room I share with my sister. They sent me toys and clothes and letters and wrote letters to Maria too.

They also prayed for me every day and missed me really badly. Sometimes my big brother Ian would get really mad at the lawyers because the paperwork takes so long and he missed me so badly. But every few months, my family would get new pictures of me and they would put them in picture frames and show all their friends and smile at what a wonderful girl I am.

My Mommy and Daddy gave me my name. Mia means "mine."

In November 2002, when I was eight months old, my Mommy and Daddy flew to Guatemala to visit me for a few days. We stayed in a nice hotel and they fed me new foods, played with me with lots of new toys, and told me all about my brothers and my sister. We had a great time. After their visit, I went back to stay with Maria for a little bit longer.

The next time I saw my Mommy and Daddy was in May 2003 when all the paperwork was done and I could finally go home with them. I said good-bye to Maria and then started a new life with my family.

We had a ride on an airplane. They gave me a panda that my brother Theo had picked out for me. When we got to Chicago, our friends and family were there with balloons and big smiles. I met my best friend Ruby that day. They were so happy to have me home and we all smiled and laughed a lot.

This is my story of how I was born in Guatemala and came home to be with my family in the US. I like my story because it's all about love. All the people in my family love each other very much. Someday my family and I want to go back to Guatemala for a visit and see the beautiful country where I was born.

● ● ●

When Mia started first grade, I worried. How would she do all day away from me? (The ego of a mother!) During preschool and kindergarten, we kept a regular schedule of half days together. We had taken mother-daughter pottery classes. We did craft projects together. She took music lessons, we ran errands and went to the library, but what she enjoyed most, according to her kindergarten journal, was "chatting with Mom" all morning.

Maybe it wasn't so much that I thought she would miss me, but I knew I'd miss her. The first grade teacher asked parents to fill in a little form about the unique gifts, challenges, and personalities of their child.

Part of what I submitted follows:

Mia is eager to learn, a hard worker and likes homework. I hope you will push her, give her challenges. She is smart and she doesn't frustrate easily. When she is frustrated, she sort of unplugs and disappears. Someday you'll chat with her and find that she has an amazing vocabulary. I think she is a dreamer. She loves to lose herself in her thoughts, loves to look at flowers, plants, and birds. Many times on summer days when my kids ran outdoors to play, I would see that she would stop short in the grass and stare at flowers, or lie on her back on a picnic bench and look at the sky. She looks, looks, looks. Sometimes I would try to stir her—"Hey go run around with your sister and brothers"—but she was content in her thoughts.

In terms of her interests, she says she would like to be a vet or a dentist someday. Both would be excellent choices for her! She had more than a dozen cavities when she got home from Guatemala and spent a lot of time at the dentist. Luckily, it was a great place and the dentist was very gentle with her. She actually loved to go. I think she would be a great visual artist too—I like what she creates and she is always drawing something.

From the first day, the teacher put her—and me—at ease. After surviving the first few weeks of school when she would walk home with Isabel, put her backpack down, and fall asleep on the couch, she did just fine. Her teacher seemed to have an appreciation for her from the start. All the kids beamed around this teacher, each seemed happy to know that he or she was the teacher's favorite student. One day after school, Mia said she needed to gather some things together for her turn as "Person of the Day." For this weeklong sort of show-and-tell, kids bring in their family pictures, talk about their favorite things, and get a little extra attention.

"What are you going to bring?"

"My special book. And the picture of my birthmother. And can I wear that Guatemala Girl T-shirt from International Night?"

The day she packed these precious things in her backpack, I worried. What if one of the other kids said something unkind to her? What if, in sharing her story, a part of it resonated in her and she felt upset at school? Remember how I learned that it wasn't me, but God who was truly caring for her, way back during the adoption process? I gave her a kiss, sent her off to school with her sister, and said a quick prayer.

God, I know You love her. I know we grow from difficult experiences. But she's so little. If this could be a positive time for her, I'd much appreciate it. But I get it: You're in control.

Late morning, I sat down at my desk and saw that I had a new e-mail message from Mia's teacher.

Monday, September 29, 2008 10:51 AM
Subject: Mia—person of the day
Hi Jen! I just wanted to let you know that Mia just shared

for her Person of the Day and it went great! The class was fascinated by her story. It was a wonderful teaching and learning experience for all of us. A lot of the kids had never heard of someone being born and then not living with their birthmother. (That was a new vocabulary word!) We loved the book! Thanks for letting Mia bring her story to us today. It was a great way to start our week together!

In the lives of each of my kids, there have been moments when I have breathed out a sigh of relief. They are times when I know, at least for a moment, that they are healthy and secure and that I have done a reasonably good job as their mother. This was one of those moments. Mia, five years after her adoption, knew her story. She desired to share it with her class and new first grade teacher. And they could understand her! That speech issue? Resolved! That deer-in-the-headlights look with new people? Gone. I put my face in my hands and had a good, long cry.

Thank You, I said.

15

Being Present

Whittier Elementary School, circa 1974. Our desks in straight rows, from the front of the classroom to the back. The tiles on the floor, each a swirl of green and gray like someone mixing paint had walked away from the job after stirring the can a few times. The smell of chalk dust and wet socks warming in polyester-lined boots. The teacher leaning on the edge of her desk, her grade book folded open to the attendance page, her pencil poised to make tiny checkmarks next to each name in the column under today's date. She begins at the top of the list and calls out our names, one by one.

A tiny flutter of excitement tightens in my chest. It's almost my turn to raise my hand and call, "Here." I love to hear my name called, to respond and affirm that I am there.

At least that's the way I remember it.

Most world religions make a big deal out of being present, as opposed to fretting over the past or fearing the future. Jews, Muslims, and Christians celebrate Sabbath, setting apart time for worship. Zen Buddhists extol the value of "nowness." Presence can be a perception that everything is all right. "It is well with my soul," the hymn says. Jesus told His followers not to be anxious. He directed their attention to lilies, "dressed in splendor" and dancing in the rain (Matthew 6:28–34).

When I was nursing Theo, my only responsibility was to feed him. The house was quiet. I breathed in his newborn smell, stroked his hair, fair and soft like corn silk, and absorbed the warmth his tiny body generated when it was pressed up against mine. Two years later, while nursing baby Ian, I read to Theo, rooted around in the toy basket next to my chair and kept him occupied, praised his block towers, and even tossed a ball with him. With Isabel, eighteen months after Ian, life was a blur. I wore her in a sling, nursed her on demand—sometimes while making dinner or pushing the older kids on the swings. I don't know how often I really focused on one sight, smell, or emotion in my life. I don't know how often I practiced "nowness," but I'm sure it never occurred to me to think about that. I was just doing my best to get by.

By the time Mia came into the family, I'd become adept at mindfulness's rival: multitasking. At first, parenting her was different from raising the other children. She didn't come to me as a tiny baby with an infant's frequent naps, inability to move about the house, and simple, straightforward needs. My new daughter was a toddler. She spoke Spanish. She struggled to walk after being carried for much of her life. She had never been told "no." My productive self rolled up its sleeves: there was much to be done.

I hesitate to offer advice to adoptive parents. I usually just tell stories about my own experience because I know I am no expert and I know people like reading stories about family. I know I do.

But there is one bit of wisdom I've earned after tripping over it too many times.

I recommend that when a child comes home, the parents make an effort simply to be present with her as much as possible. Not just in the room, but truly present. Try not to fret over your adopted child's past, much of which will always be a mystery to you. Don't fear the future. Spend time with people who celebrate your child. Go on walks with her; when she's old enough, give her blank paper and crayons and watch her make drawings. She will show something about herself to you in what she creates on that page. Quietly explore with her as she gets to know a world that is very new to her.

I wish I'd done more of those things with Mia early on after her homecoming. I was so eager to speed her through the acclimation process, I think I failed to just sit and appreciate her as much as I should have. I wanted her to "catch up." I was eager to prove wrong the people who expressed concern about my adopting her—those who told me horror stories about troubled adopted children, who wondered aloud whether she would be close to her siblings, who lamented that she wouldn't compare favorably with my older three. In my heart, I knew these cynics were wrong (and indeed time has shown that they were), but instead of releasing their negative comments, I set out—for a time—to prove them wrong.

Now that my little daughter is a happy, thriving member of the family, I find myself spending much more time just being with her. We look at the autumn leaves. We read books. We laugh together at her silly jokes.

I enjoy her presence, and my own.

And loving her makes me want to be present for others too.

If I've learned anything since adopting Mia, it is that trying to control the opinions of others is a fruitless pursuit. I can't control what others think of her. I can't protect her from people who may say something insensitive to her about her adoption. I can't help it that some people will only see the color of her skin when they look at my daughter.

Adopting Mia brought my own limitations out into the light. I want to be liked too much. I doubt myself too much. I fear the disapproval of others too much. I coddle myself, lick my wounds, and I don't trust in God's love for me the way I should. I am quick to forgive others, slow to forgive myself. It's torn off the veneer and helped me live a little more honestly—which is to say, of course, that it's made my life harder.

I recently corresponded with a pastor who seems to grasp God's love more than almost anyone I have ever met. At the end of one of his e-mail messages, he wrote words that took me by surprise, filled my eyes with tears, and made my heart do a little flip-flop:

> God loves you, Jennifer, with an everlasting love. His love never changes, loving you on your worst day as much as He does on your best day.

I was standing outdoors at a gas station as my tank filled, reading his e-mail on my mobile phone. *Oh I wish I could truly believe that, even for a second,* I thought. *Why do I believe it for others and not for myself?*

Later that week, I wrote him back and thanked him for his words. I admitted that accepting that God loves me is a challenge. I didn't get all literary in my e-mail with him, discussing the metaphor of Dr. T. J. Eckleburg in *The Great Gatsby*. Nor did I tell him my sad story of growing up without a father and repeatedly hearing how God was loving, "just like our earthly fathers." I just wrote, "Your message of God's love is a salve to my heart. To hear that, really hear it, is just what I need spiritually."

I didn't expect a response, especially one that would again bring me to tears and open what had felt like a locked—or at least jammed—door in my heart. But I got one.

> So I'll tell you again how much God loves you but in different words. You are precious to God, Jen. So completely cherished by Him it is absolutely amazing. He delights in you exactly as you are. His love is never tied to performance. He always loves you perfectly, without holding anything back. You are the apple of His eye.

● ● ●

About eight years after the fact, when the rest of the family was out, Mia and I sat at our kitchen counter and watched the DVD of the first visit David and I made to Guatemala. The first clips were taken in our hotel room. She sat on the bed in her onesie, her eyes wide; her lime green dress that I was so eager to change her out of is nowhere to be seen. David was filming us and I gave him directions and commented on the way she was playing with her new toys, a stacking game and Peter Rabbit doll.

In a fit of creativity while watching the DVD, Mia started an impromptu voiceover and I joined her.

MIA: "Who is this lady? I don't understand anything she's saying to me. Can't she speak Spanish?"

JEN: "Oh, look at her chubby little legs. She looks healthy. I think she's really doing all right."

MIA: "Why is she squeezing my legs? Hey, stop it. That tickles. And anyway, where am I? I've never been in here before."

JEN: "Oh, I hope she loves me. Does she love me? Will she ever love me?"

Mia stopped her performance suddenly and turned to me. "What? Really? You were thinking *that*?"

"I was," I said.

We watched to the end of the DVD. We laughed at the extended peekaboo game the three of us played at the hotel restaurant with those big linen napkins. We paused to look at the volcano that I'd filmed, in the distance, from our hotel balcony.

When the movie was done, I asked her if she was okay.

"Yeah," she said. She was obviously puzzled. A crease divided her forehead. "What do you mean?"

"It doesn't upset you, thinking about that time?"

"No—why would it?" she asked.

"I don't know," I said. "I guess because it was an in-between time. You weren't in our family yet, but you were. I guess *I* feel upset remembering it."

"Weird," she said, shrugging her shoulders. "Hey can we start our movie now? We could watch *High Society*." She chose my favorite movie, trying to cheer me up. A few minutes later, we were snuggled on the couch, singing along with Louis Armstrong.

● ● ●

At the end of *About Schmidt*, as Warren guides his RV home after a long road trip, we hear his final letter to Ndugu. In it, he acknowledges—Ecclesiastes-style—the insignificance of all people, but he says that maybe the best we can hope for is to make a difference in other people's lives. Warren, however, says his life hasn't made a difference. He hasn't made anyone's life better.

Warren finally acknowledges to his only friend that, unlike Walt Disney or Buffalo Bill Cody or the other men he admires, he is not remarkable. He is dust and to dust he shall return. He returns to his empty house and to the pile of mail that is waiting for him there. One is from Tanzania. A nun has written on behalf of Ndugu, whom, she explains, is illiterate. She politely thanks Warren for his letters and says she has read them to the boy, who has enjoyed receiving them. She indicates that because of Warren's financial support, she has been able to get much-needed medical care for Ndugu. Now he is thriving. Warren finishes reading the letter and then turns to the next page of the letter. On it he finds a drawing that Ndugu has made for him. It's a picture of himself with Warren, side by side and holding hands.

It's at that point in the movie when you realize that Nicholson hasn't smiled a real smile as Warren Schmidt in the entire movie. Looking at Ndugu's drawing, Warren smiles a smile so pure and transcendent that you're certain that Warren Schmidt understands his life has indeed been vitally important to another person.[1]

It did matter that he was here.

Opening yourself to an orphaned child may not save the world, but it might save one precious life. And the miracle is that the life you save may be your own.[2]

Epilogue:

"She call you 'Mom'?"

A few weeks ago, my daughters and I took a detour on our way to the grocery store to get manicures. The women at the nail salon are Vietnamese and often do not speak to clients while they work. They chat together and glance over at a laptop that gets crystal-clear programming from a Vietnamese television station. I like going there, hearing the women speak to each other and seeing glimpses of Hanoi or the countryside when I'm near enough to see the screen of the laptop. There is also a television in the salon that plays trashy American shows. This one, ironically, gets terrible reception. Through the static and lines, it's possible to follow the story of whatever program is on because the closed captioning function is always turned on.

Mia, Isabel, and I walked into the salon, quite pleased with ourselves for making this spontaneous field trip. My daughters, now eight and ten, stood at the racks of polish for a long time and considered their choices. I was directed to sit down at a nail station and complied, straining to hear my daughters' chirpy conversation several feet away over the sound of the competing television shows. *The People's Court* was on the American television.

"Do you like 'Ogre-the-Top Blue' or 'Teal the Cows Come Home'?" Mia asked.

"That one's better," Isabel said, with big sister authority.

"Ogre-the-Top Blue," Mia said. "Yeah. You're right."

Isabel grabbed three bottles from the rack. "I like these," she said to no one in particular. "But I can't decide between 'Black Cherry Chutney' and 'Lincoln Park at Midnight.'"

"You've got to choose, girls," I said. I always end up saying that. I spoke loudly so they could hear me over *The People's Court*.

"Coming!" Mia said, ever the fourth child, ever eager to please. She walked over and stood beside me.

"Just a second," Isabel said, grabbing a few more bottles from the rack.

The woman who was clipping my nails looked up and pointed at Mia.

"She you daughter?" the woman asked, pointing the clippers at Mia.

"Yes," I said.

"I'm not sure about the Ogre one. What about this?" Mia asked, turning the bottle over. "It's 'Yodel Me on My Cell.'"

"It's fun," I said.

Isabel joined us. "I'm ready. This is it: 'Mrs. O'Leary's BBQ,'" she said.

"Ooh. Creepy," I said, thinking of the song we learned growing up in the suburbs of Chicago. I started to sing it to them, "Ol' Mother Leary left the lantern in the shed, and when the cow kicked it over, she winked her eye and said, 'It'll be a hot time in the old town tonight . . .'"

Mia laughed; Isabel looked around the salon to make sure no one else could hear us.

"Mo-om," she said, making it a two-syllable word.

"It's about the Chicago Fire," I said.

Mia sat beside me and started spinning her chair around.

"Step?" the woman asked me, pointing at Mia again.

"Pardon me?" I asked.

"Step? She you *step*daughter?"

"No, she's my daughter," I said.

"You daughter?" the woman looked confused. She put down the cuticle cutter.

"I adopted her when she was a baby."

Mia smiled. Everyone likes hearing a reference to their own babyhoods. Isn't it true?

"Mexico?" the woman asked. "She from Mexico?"

"No," I said, hoping I'd chosen my nail color correctly. I liked "Nomad's Dream," but wondered if a pinker "Rosy Future" was better. There was still time to change it. I hadn't even had the hand massage yet.

The woman pointed at Mia's arms and said, "She dark."

"She was born in Guatemala." I straightened in my chair, suddenly aware that this conversation wasn't ending anytime soon. I glanced at Mia and wondered whether it bothered her or whether she really was as interested in the staticky Dr. Pepper commercial as she seemed.

"Iz-bel. Iz-bel," Mia called to her sister who had returned to the nail polish. "Iz-a-bell. Dr. Pepper!"

Isabel cheered.

"Mexico?" the woman asked. It occurred to me if Germany is Deutschland to the Germans, Allemagne to the French, and

Germany to us, what do they call Guatemala in Vietnam? Maybe the nail polish fumes were getting to me, but I became lost in thought over this question. "Guatemala is a country *south* of Mexico. In Latin America," I said.

I glanced over at Mia, who continued to smile a patient, beatific smile.

"How long you got her?" the woman asked, but before I could answer, she stood up and walked to the counter. Another customer had walked into the salon.

"Sign here," she said to the person who had entered, tapping on a clipboard.

"I've got you forever," I whispered to Mia. She laughed.

"She lucky," the woman said when she returned to my hands. She lowered her voice. "When she sixteen year old, you tell her you adopt her."

"She knows she was adopted," I said. "We talk about it. And, you know what, I am the lucky one. I'm lucky to be her mother."

Isabel was spinning Mia's chair around and I tried to see if Mia had heard me. If over the blaring television and the ugly tale of a used mattress being sold as new on *The People's Court* and the sound of the nail dryers and the water filling a tub for someone's pedicure and the Vietnamese program from the computer, I hoped she was listening.

"Mimi! Mimi—look. It's the Geiko gecko," Isabel shouted, pointing at the television.

"Oh yeah!" Mia said.

"She call you 'Mom'?" the woman asked. Her voice was tender now, curious.

"Yes I call her Mom," Mia said. "'Cause she's my mom."

I blew her a little kiss and Mia stood up, leaned toward me, and put her forehead against mine. A wordless show of affection we'd been doing for years. She then went and sat down again and started spinning her chair around again.

"Go wash hands," the woman said to me. "Then we do color."

Tips for Prospective Adoptive Parents

If you are considering adoption, here are a few tips to keep in mind.

Before You Begin

- Acknowledge your real (as in authentic, not glossed-over) feelings to friends and family. It's normal to experience a sense of loss after a difficult series of infertility treatments. It's normal for your feelings to fluctuate between excitement and uncertainty at the thought of adopting a child.
- Remember that, just like a marriage begins after the wedding ceremony, the adoption process is only the precursor to raising a child and creating a family.

During the Adoption Process

- Choose an agency *after* doing careful research on its ethics, history, and other elements. See organizations such as Parents for Ethical Adoption Reform (pear-now.org) to learn about good agencies and much more.

- Don't stress out over the home visit. (No one will check the dates on the bottles of salad dressing in your fridge.)
- Don't accept a referral of a child with medical issues unless you have researched worst-case scenarios thoroughly. *Read* every book and article you can get your hands on. *Talk* with parents who are raising children with that special need. *Be honest* with yourself about whether you feel prepared financially and emotionally to address these issues.
- Be authentic with yourself, your spouse, and your social worker about whether you are willing to become a "conspicuous family" by adopting a child of another race or with special needs that may draw the attention of strangers wherever you go.
- Don't look at an agency's photo listing unless it is the agency with which you *already have* a relationship. The pitfalls associated with falling in love with a child on a waiting child photo listing are many.
- Try to be proactive while you wait. Spend quality time with other children in the family. Invest in your relationship with your spouse. Finish college credits or complete other long-delayed projects.
- From the time you decide to adopt, engage with other adoptive parents. Join a support group; attend cultural events geared toward families who have adopted children. Create community so that when you have concerns, joys, or questions to share later in the process, you have a built-in network of supporters.

- Read *The Post-Adoption Blues* by Karen Foli and John Thompson (listed in Resources section of this book) during your wait. But don't give it away when you are done—revisit it again a few months after your child has come home. Be honest about your fears, failings, and questions with other adoptive parents and professionals.

- During the adoption process, get to know what is "normal" for children at different developmental stages. Ask your doctor or child's pediatrician (or buy a book such as *What to Expect the First Year*) and get to know how babies and children typically develop. If your child has lived in a less-than-optimal environment, give him or her time to catch up.

- Create a file (or shoebox) in which you drop airplane ticket stubs, hotel stationery, foreign restaurant checks, or other souvenirs of your trip to meet your new child, if applicable. Later you will be glad to have these physical reminders of your first days together for scrapbooks, Lifebooks, and other projects.

- Write down your questions for your child's caregiver, if applicable. In the moment of meeting your child and having your child placed in your arms, it's hard to remember to ask questions you later might wish to have asked, such as "What comforts her when she is sad?" or "Does she have favorite songs or games?" or "What do you feel is special or different about her?" These details of his or her early life will also be helpful when you make a Lifebook for your child.

After Your Child Has Come Home

- Limit visits from family and friends for the first few weeks. If you are adopting a baby, your pediatrician may recommend that you limit guests to reduce chances for infections. An older child, after coming home, needs time to know that you are his or her new parents. Meeting many new people in his or her first days home might be upsetting or confusing.
- Talk openly with your child about his or her adoption. Adoption was the way you and your child were brought together. It's not a secret, so hushed tones are not necessary.
- Add children's books to your collection that celebrate adoptive families (see Resources section for suggestions).
- Make a Lifebook for your child and record all the details of what caregivers told you about his or her early life. Do it while it's all fresh in your mind—these details will be of great value to your child.
- Be present with your child. Enjoy your child. Play games you loved as a child. Sing songs you loved. Teach her how to eat Oreos!
- Remember that your child is a gift from God and is counting on you for love, patience, and security.

Discussion Questions

1. At the beginning of the book, Grant writes that "Families are ever in process, ducking and taking cover during times of grief and hardship and casually strolling through easier times, forgetting to notice how fortunate they are. On ordinary days, as well as on life-changing ones, just when we think we know what our lives are like, things change. We scramble to figure out what will be the new normal from then on."

   In what ways has becoming a parent—or starting the adoption process—"upended" your life? Have you experienced moments when you knew that everything has changed? How did they make you feel?

2. "After all, the decision to adopt was not my idea, really. I was merely responding to a tap on the shoulder from God. I was sure of it. Wouldn't God, then, expedite the whole thing? I knew God could."

   Have you ever experience a "calling," or what you knew to be a divine "tap on the shoulder"? Did responding to that nudge ultimately make your life easier or more difficult? Were you surprised by the way things turned out?

3. Grant writes that she expected her adopted toddler somehow to be mature beyond her years and aware of

all Grant and her family went through to adopt her. Have you ever placed unrealistic expectations on your children? On yourself?

4. Although the author didn't experience infertility herself, she writes at length about journeying through her best friend's IVF treatments and grief over infertility. What's the most difficult thing you've had to help a friend endure? Are there people whom you can call on to be with you at your lowest times?

5. How do you reconcile the belief that God is good with the fact that so many children live in abject poverty? Do you agree with World Vision US president Richard Sterns that helping the poor is your responsibility?

6. Early on in the book, Grant writes about her husband's depression when, before having children, he felt his career was stalled. She, meanwhile, was in a bright time in her life. Have you ever been in a moment when you and your spouse are in very different places emotionally? What helped you come through that time? What was most difficult about it?

7. "I didn't feel God's presence, but I chose to believe God was with me. It wasn't the first time that was true, nor was it the last. I once heard a priest say, 'That's why it's called faith. You don't see it on this side, but you decide to believe. It's not a feeling, but an action, a choice.'" Do you always feel aware of God's presence with you? If not, how do you "keep the faith" in those dry times? What is your advice to others who find themselves feeling disconnected from their spiritual lives?

8. Beginning in the chapter entitled, "Parenting Genius,

Dethroned," Grant admits that her confidence, certainty, and high standards of parenting crumbled over time. If you are a parent, what events in your life or the life of your child humbled you? If you are planning to be a parent, do you ever think, *When I'm a parent, I'll never* _____? *(Feed him fast food? Allow her to watch TV? Have a child who whines?)*

9. One theme in *Love You More* is that life continuously changes. Are you comfortable with this—or do you wish you could make it stop and hold still? How do you manage your feelings about change?

10. Near the end of the book, Grant invokes the movie *About Schmidt*. Of the character Warren Schmidt, she writes that he is "a recently widowed insurance agent who, increasingly, becomes aware of the meaninglessness of his life." But at the end of the movie, when he looks at Ndugu's drawing, Schmidt realizes "his life has indeed been vitally important to another person." Does the resolution of Warren Schmidt's loneliness and questioning mirror the story told in *Love You More*? Why or why not?

Resources

Adoption

Recommended adoption placement, funding, and educational organizations

Adoption-Link/adoption-link.org

This Oak Park, Illinois, adoption agency "provides quality services for all in the adoption triad: birth parents, children, and adoptive families. We specialize in domestic and international adoption and humanitarian services for African, African-American, multiracial, HIV+ and other special needs children. We believe that all children have a right to loving and permanent homes."

Dave Thomas Foundation for Adoption/davethomasfoundation.org

This foundation, according to the website, "exists to be an agent of change in the lives of children in North America waiting to be adopted out of foster care and in the attitudes of adults who, either unknowingly or helplessly, allow children to linger in government systems without the birthright of every child—a safe, loving and permanent family."

Evan B. Donaldson Foundation/adoptioninstitute.org

The Adoption Institute's mission is "to provide leadership that improves adoption laws, policies and practices—through sound research, education and advocacy—in order to better the lives of everyone touched by adoption."

Show Hope Foundation/showhope.org

Show Hope is a nonprofit organization that mobilizes individuals and communities to meet the most pressing needs of orphans in distress by providing 1) homes for waiting children through adoption aid grants, and 2) life-saving medical care for orphans with special needs.

Humanitarian Relief and Development

These organizations promote health, education, and justice to some of the world's most vulnerable people, including orphans.

Action International/actionintl.org

Action International Ministries (ACTION) is a global mission agency committed to sending multinational missionaries who treasure Jesus Christ and minister His gospel in word and deed, primarily to the poor. Missionaries such as Susanna and Thomas Smoak serve street children in Latin American countries by rescuing abandoned children, working to reunite children with relatives. They also work to develop a foster care network rooted in local churches and to support needy families in high-risk areas of Sao Paulo.

Chikumbuso/chikumbuso.org

Begun in 2005 by Linda Wilkinson, an American woman in

Zambia who hoped to support one widow and seven orphaned children, the Chikumbuso project now serves hundreds of people impacted by the HIV/AIDS pandemic by providing refuge for abused children, job training for widows and single mothers, and nutrition and education for hundreds of orphaned children.

Doctors Without Borders/doctorswithoutborders.org

Doctors Without Borders delivers medical help to populations endangered by war, civil strife, epidemics, or natural disasters. Doctors work worldwide in front-line hospitals, refugee camps, disaster sites, towns, and villages providing primary health care, performing surgery, vaccinating children, operating emergency nutrition and sanitation programs, and training local medical staff.

PATH/path.org

PATH is an international nonprofit organization that creates sustainable, culturally relevant solutions, enabling communities worldwide to break longstanding cycles of poor health. PATH helps to provide appropriate health technologies and vital strategies to improve global health and well-being.

Saddleback Church Orphan Care Connection/ orphansandthechurch.com

"Saddleback Church has chosen to make the care of orphans and vulnerable children a signature issue of our church. We are providing meaningful ways for every person to engage in caring for orphans through local churches at home and around the world. If you're exploring adoption or foster care internationally or domestically, we're ready to serve you."

World Bicycle Relief/worldbicyclerelief.org

People in underdeveloped regions of the world are suffering

every day due to lack of access to health care, education, and economic development opportunities. Bicycles are simple, sustainable, and appropriate technology to support people in developing nations and disaster recovery. The mission of World Bicycle Relief is to provide access to independence and livelihood through the Power of Bicycles.

World Vision/worldvision.org

World Vision is a Christian humanitarian organization dedicated to working with children, families, and their communities worldwide to reach their full potential by tackling the causes of poverty and injustice. World Vision's "Empowerment, Respect, and Equality Project" improves the well-being of girls and women in Zambia through academic scholarships, loans, and business training.

Books about Adoption

Simon, Scott. *Baby, We Were Meant for Each Other: In Praise of Adoption.* New York: Random House, 2010.

Chapman, Mary Beth, Steven Curtis Chapman, and Ellen Vaughn. *Choosing to SEE: A Journey of Struggle and Hope.* New York: Revell, 2010.

O'Toole, Elisabeth. *In on It: What Adoptive Parents Would Like You to Know About Adoption. A Guide for Relatives and Friends.* New York: Fig Press, 2010.

Horner, Susan and Kelly Fordyce Martindale. *Loved by Choice: True Stories That Celebrate Adoption.* New York: Revell, 2002.

O'Dwyer, Jessica. *Mamalita: An Adoption Memoir.* Berkeley, CA: Seal Press, 2010.

Watkins, Mary and Susan Fisher. *Talking with Young Children about Adoption*. New Haven, CT: Yale University Press, 1995.

Pavao, Joyce Maguire. *The Family of Adoption*. Boston: Beacon Press, 2005.

Foli, Karen J. and John R. Thompson. *The Post-Adoption Blues: Overcoming the Unforeseen Challenges of Adoption*. New York: Rodale, 2004.

Hopkins-Best, Mary. *Toddler Adoption: The Weaver's Craft*. Indianapolis: Perspectives Press, 1998.

Books and Websites about Parenting and Family Life

Currey-Wilson, Ellen. *The Big Turnoff: Confessions of a TV-Addicted Mom Trying to Raise a T.V.-Free Kid*. Chapel Hill, NC: Algonquin Books, 2007.

eatdinner.org (research, education, and resources on the benefits of eating dinner with your family)

Skenazy, Lenore. *Free-Range Kids, How to Raise Safe, Self-Reliant Children (Without Going Nuts with Worry)*. New York: Jossey-Bass, 2010. www.freerangekids.com.

Christopher, Todd. *The Green Hour: A Daily Dose of Nature for Happier, Healthier, Smarter Kids*. Boston: Trumpeter, 2010.

inspiringmoms.com (online tools to find "greater balance, success, and happiness in motherhood")

Cohen, Lawrence J. *Playful Parenting*. New York: Ballantine, 2002.

Gottman, John, Joan Declaire, and Daniel Goleman. *Raising an Emotionally Intelligent Child: The Heart of Parenting*. New York: Simon & Schuster, 1998.

Sears, William, Martha Sears, and Elizabeth Pantley. *The Successful Child: What Parents Can Do to Help Kids Turn Out Well.* New York: Little, Brown, and Company, 2002.

Mellor, Christie. *The Three-Martini Playdate: A Practical Guide to Happy Parenting.* San Francisco: Chronicle Books, 2004.

Books for Children

Kasza, Keiko. *A Mother for Choco.* New York: Putnam Juvenile, 1996.

Lamperti, Noelle. *Brown Like Me.* Norwich, VT: Victoria Publishers, 1999.

Kitze, Carrie A. *I Don't Have Your Eyes.* Warren, NJ: EMK Press, 2003.

Lewis, Rose A. *I Love You Like Crazy Cakes.* New York: Little, Brown Young Readers, 2000.

Pellegrini, Nina. *Families Are Different.* New York: Holiday House, 1991.

Rogers, Fred. *Let's Talk About It: Adoption.* New York: Putnam Juvenile, 1998.

Schreck, Karen Halvorsen. *Lucy's Family Tree.* Gardiner, ME: Tilbury House, 2006.

Gill, Jim. *May There Always Be Sunshine.* Oak Park, IL: Jim Gill, 2001.

Curtis, Jamie Lee. *Tell Me Again About the Night I Was Born.* New York: HarperCollins, 1996.

Lucado, Max. *You Are Special.* Wheaton, IL: Crossway, 1997.

Notes

A Conspicuous Family

1. Danielle Friedman, "Making Adoption Work," *The Daily Beast*, World News, http://www.thedailybeast.com/blogs-and-stories/2010-11-17/women-in-the-world-fixing-the-adoption-crisis/; see also NumberOf.net, "Orphans in the World," http://www.numberof.net/orphans-in-the-world.

1. Mowing the Lawn in the Dark

1. Caryn Dahlstrand Rivadeneira, *Mama's Got a Fake I.D.* (Colorado Springs: WaterBrook, 2009), 4.

3. Parenting Genius, Dethroned

1. Carolyn Nystrom, *Before You Were Born (God's Design for Sex)* (Colorado Springs: NavPress, 1997); Ruth S. Hummel, *Where Do Babies Come From?* (New York: Concordia, 1998).
2. Max Lucado, *You Are Special* (Wheaton, IL: Crossway, 1997).

4. The Red Thread

1. Max Lucado, *You Are Special* (Wheaton, IL: Crossway, 1997).
2. Richard Stearns, *The Hole in Our Gospel* (Nashville: Thomas Nelson, 2009), 123.
3. Lucinda Vardey, comp., *Mother Teresa: A Simple Path* (New York: Ballantine, 1995), 80.

5. A Whisper

1. Book of Common Prayer, "Holy Baptism," http://www.bookofcommonprayer.net/holy_baptism.php.
2. Pam Blackburn, e-mail to author, October 2010.
3. Margaret Fleming, interview with author, December 14, 2009. For more information on Adoption-Link, Inc., see http://www.adoptionlink.org.
4. Jennifer Grant, "Adoption agency helps place children with HIV," *Chicago Tribune*, January 6, 2010, http://articles.chicagotribune.

com/2010-01-06/news/1001040063_1_hiv-positive-hiv-tests-newborns. © January 6, 2010, *Chicago Tribune*. All rights reserved. Used by permission. The printing, copying, redistribution, or retransmission of the material without express written permission is prohibited.

5. UNICEF, "Children and AIDS," www.unicef.org/publications/files/CATSR_EN_11202008.pdf.

6. Grant, "Adoption agency helps place children with HIV."

7. Ibid.

8. Margaret Fleming, interview with the author.

9. Grant, "Adoption agency helps place children with HIV."

10. Ibid.

6. Where in the World Would We Find Her?

1. Lenore Skenazy: "America's 'Worst Mom'?" *The New York Sun*, April 8, 2008, http://www.nysun.com/opinion/americas-worst-mom/74347.

2. Lenore Skenazy, Free-Range Kids: How to Raise Safe, Self-Reliant Children (Without Going Nuts with Worry) blog, "About Free Range," http://freerangekids.wordpress.com/about-2.

3. Steve Bradshaw, "Struggling with India's Gender Bias," BBC News, August 19, 2008, http://news.bbc.co.uk/2/hi/7570192.stm. See also http://www.gendercide.org/case_infanticide.html.

7. Adoption: A Crime, a Necessary Evil, or a Miracle?

1. UNICEF, Press Centre, "UNICEF's Position on Inter-country Adoption," http://www.unicef.org/media/media_41118.html.

2. AdoptUsKids, "About the Children in Foster Care," http://www.adoptuskids.org/resourceCenter/aboutTheChildren.aspx.

3. Arthur Brice, contributor, "Guatemalan army stole children for adoption, report says," CNN, September 12, 2009, http://www.cnn.com/2009/WORLD/americas/09/12/guatemala.child.abduction/index.html.

4. Laurie Stern, "Nine Months in Guatemala," Americas.org, 2000, available at http://www.bluecollaradoption.com/2006/09/interesting-article-i-wanted-to-pass.html.

5. Ibid.

6. Garrison Keillor's *A Prairie Home Companion*, American Public Media, http://prairiehome.publicradio.org/about/podcast.

7. Laurie Stern, e-mail to the author, October 17, 2010.

8. Civil Liberties Act of 1988, Pub.L. 100-383, title I, August 10, 1988, 102 Stat. 904, 50a U.S.C. § 1989b et seq.

9. The Waiting Is the Hardest Part

1. John Donne, *Holy Sonnets*, XIV, lines 1–4, in *Poems of John Donne*, vol. I, E. K. Chambers, ed. (London: Lawrence & Bullen, 1896), 165.

11. Honeymooners

1. *About Schmidt*, director/writer: Alexander Payne, Jim Taylor; from the novel by Louis Begley; cinematographer: James Glennon; editor: Kevin Tent; music: Rolfe Kent; starring Jack Nicholson (Warren Schmidt), Runtime: 125; MPAA Rating: R; producers: Harry Gittes/Michael Besman (Los Angeles: New Line Cinema; 2002).

13. Tummy Ladies and Other Kinds of Mothers

1. Mary Watkins and Susan Fisher, MD, *Talking to Young Children about Adoption* (New Haven, CT: Yale University Press, 1995).

14. Her Story

1. Joseph Addison, "Ode," lines 9–12, in *The Spectator* (London: J. and R. Tonson, 1712).

15. Being Present

1. *About Schmidt*, director/writer: Alexander Payne (Los Angeles: New Line Cinema; 2002).

2. Flannery O'Connor, "The Life You Save May Be Your Own," in *Flannery O'Connor: Collected Works : Wise Blood / A Good Man Is Hard to Find / The Violent Bear It Away / Everything that Rises Must Converge / Essays & Letters* (New York: Library of America, 1988), 172.

About the Author

Jennifer Grant is a journalist whose columns, feature stories, and blog posts have been published in *Sun-Times Media* newspapers, *Christiantiy Today*, her.meneutics—a blog for women, and adoption.com. Jennifer writes a column for the *Chicago Tribune*. She is a member of the National Society of Newspaper Columnists and is a founding member of Redbud Writers Guild. Jennifer lives in the Chicago suburbs with her husband and four children and has expertise in throwing parties, traveling light, and daydreaming.

More at jennifergrant.com.

Grant/Love You More - 93

LaVergne, TN USA
14 March 2011
219962LV00004B/2/P